# POPULATION POLICY AND THE U.S. CONSTITUTION

# KLUWER·NIJHOFF STUDIES IN HUMAN ISSUES:

*An International Series in the Social Sciences*

This series is devoted to books by qualified scholars that deal with national or international themes from a variety of social science disciplines. It is intended to serve as a bridge of information between the academic community and those serving as policymakers. Furthermore, the series is intended to stimulate debate as well as to point out areas where further social science research is needed.

# POPULATION POLICY AND THE U.S. CONSTITUTION

**Larry D. Barnett**
*Widener University*

*With a Foreword by*
**Kurt W. Back**
*Duke University*

**Kluwer • Nijhoff Publishing**
*Boston/The Hague/London*

DISTRIBUTORS FOR NORTH AMERICA:
Kluwer Boston, Inc.
190 Old Derby Street
Hingham, Massachusetts 02043, U.S.A.

DISTRIBUTORS OUTSIDE NORTH AMERICA:
Kluwer Academic Publishers Group
Distribution Centre
P.O. Box 322
3300 AH Dordrecht, The Netherlands

**Library of Congress Cataloging in Publication Data**

Barnett, Larry D.
  Population policy and the U.S. Constitution.

  (Kluwer • Nijhoff studies in human issues)
  Includes index.
  1. Population—Law and legislation—United States.  2. United States—Population policy.
I. Title.  II. Series.
KF3771.B37    344.73'048    81-15579
ISBN 0-89838-082-0    347.30448    AACR2

Copyright © 1982 by Kluwer • Nijhoff Publishing

No part of this book may be reproduced in any form by print, photoprint, microfilm, or any other means without written permission from the publisher.

Printed in the United States of America

# CONTENTS

Foreword by Kurt W. Back ... ix

Preface ... xv

## I LEGAL DIMENSIONS OF THE POPULATION ISSUE

**1 Introduction** ... 3
   Demographic Sources of U.S. Population Growth ... 4
   Population Growth and Constitutional Law ... 7
   Notes ... 8

**2 Population and Law** ... 11
   Family Planning and Population Size ... 12
   Law and the Population Perspective ... 14
   Legislation Stemming from Population Growth ... 17
   Notes ... 33

**3 Population Growth and the Right of Privacy** ... 41
   Constitutional Right of Privacy ... 41
   Cases Involving Population Growth and the
      Right of Privacy ... 42

|  |  | Tort Law and the Right of Privacy | 46 |
|---|---|---|---|
|  |  | Energy Shortages and the Right of Privacy | 47 |
|  |  | Notes | 48 |

## II  SOME FACTORS AFFECTING CHILDBEARING

|  |  |  |  |
|---|---|---|---|
|  | 4 | Constitutional Law and "the Tragedy of the Commons" | 53 |
|  |  | Private Ownership and the Protection of Resources | 54 |
|  |  | Constitutional Protection against the Burdens of Children | 56 |
|  |  | Childrearing and Sex Roles | 64 |
|  |  | Notes | 69 |
|  | 5 | Legal Protection and Female Employment | 75 |
|  |  | Congressional Powers over Sex Discrimination | 76 |
|  |  | Judicial Powers over Sex Discrimination | 78 |
|  |  | Conclusions and Implications regarding Fertility | 88 |
|  |  | Notes | 90 |
|  | 6 | Housing Policies Prohibiting Children | 99 |
|  |  | State Action | 100 |
|  |  | Due Process and Equal Protection | 101 |
|  |  | Notes | 106 |

## III  FERTILITY CONTROL POLICIES: SOME POSSIBILITIES

|  |  |  |  |
|---|---|---|---|
|  | 7 | Government Regulation of Sexual Relationships | 113 |
|  |  | Establishment of a Minimum Age for Marriage | 115 |
|  |  | Regulation of Nonmarital Relationships | 118 |
|  |  | Notes | 122 |
|  | 8 | Taxation and the Control of Fertility | 125 |
|  |  | Forms of Taxation to Reduce Population Growth | 126 |
|  |  | Constitutionality of a Fertility Control Tax | 130 |
|  |  | Notes | 136 |
|  | 9 | Tuition in the Public Schools | 141 |
|  |  | Constitutionality of Tuition Charges | 142 |

|     | Congressional Action to Establish a Tuition System | 146 |
|     | Notes | 148 |

## IV TWO CONTEMPORARY CONTROVERSIAL ISSUES

**10 Abortion** — 151
    Right of Privacy — 152
    Responsibility of Physicians — 154
    Viability of the Fetus — 155
    Consent of Other Persons — 156
    Government Funding of Abortion for Indigent Women — 159
    Notes — 162

**11 Immigration** — 165
    Congressional Authority over Immigration — 165
    Illegal Aliens — 173
    Notes — 174

**Afterword** — 177
    Notes — 179

**Index** — 181

# FOREWORD

A few decades ago a monograph on the legal aspects of population control would have looked mainly at legal prohibitions. The salient legal problems were restriction of the use of birth control and dissemination of information about it. The assumption in such an approach would have been that effective population control is legally affected only by the clearly stated restrictions in the law. In other respects, the law could be assumed to be neutral.

Judicial and legislative changes have eliminated practically all restrictions on the means of contraception. This development, however, has not freed population from its relation to the law; on the contrary, it has exposed the importance of law as a motivating force for and against population control. Although much applied work in population control is directed toward the distribution of contraceptives, concentration on the means of population control has shown itself to be of doubtful value. From many sides the primary importance of motivation has been recognized, along with the need to influence motivation and to analyze the conditions under which motivational change is possible. At this point the role of the law becomes apparent, along with the recognition that law has not been neutral in this issue — that, in fact, it cannot be neutral.

Larry Barnett has undertaken a pioneering effort in identifying the areas of law important to changing people's motivations in regard to population control and to a reduction in individual family size. He has focused unflinchingly on this issue and has accepted some results that may be uncomfortable for many interests. His work clearly opens a new stage in the history of population control as a political and social issue.

The topics discussed in the book, as well as the general field of population policy, have become centers of controversy and heated political discussion. The book is a product of this controversy and is likely to be an important new contribution to political discussion. Therefore, one must look at the complex network of allies and opponents in the field of population policy. For some time interest in population planning has been a mainstay of traditional liberal concerns, which include civil rights, women's rights, increased government support of welfare, sexual permissiveness, and cooperation with the Third World. In regard to population control, some conflicts exist within these seemingly equally worthy groups: Minority groups are sometimes afraid that population policies are directed at them; while women's groups may feel that women's control over their own bodies justifies abortion, they would be leery of unrestricted sterilization. But, in general, attitudes favoring population control have been found in traditional liberal coalitions. Even more important, organizations have become important partners in coalitions to promote each other's aims.

One may speculate on how far these coalitions have influenced the course of population policy. They may have been an important influence on the concentration on family planning instead of on the larger perspective of population control, at least as far as practical measures were concerned. Emphasis on the freedom of sale, publicizing, and prescription of contraceptives or on sex education was in line with the emphasis on civil liberties and progressive child rearing to which all the groups in this loose coalition subscribed. The groups argued against their opposition by pointing out that family-planning policies only enlarged people's freedom of choice and did not try to influence them away from their basic values.

# FOREWORD

Emphasis on family planning has worked only up to a certain point. There were people who had more children than they wanted, primarily because of lack of knowledge and access to effective contraception; helping them did decrease fertility. However, as a serious solution to overpopulation, the family-planning approach is not sufficient. If it is universally assumed that the policy of the state is to encourage and facilitate childbearing, then provision of means for birth control will not solve the population problem. One must look at the social institutions, assess whether they influence population increase, and investigate how they could be changed.

Experience with a purely family-planning approach has shown that the social control mechanisms, including law, are not neutral in influencing motivation for population control. One has to look beyond the ever-popular "quick fix" of better contraceptive techniques to assess expression of population policies in the basic values of the society—for instance, as expressed in the Constitution and in its interpretation by the courts. Professor Barnett is a pioneer in looking at the foundations of population policy and the consequences of a consistent position. He states explicitly that population control is such a crucial concern that definite steps must be taken to promote it—not just persuasion but, if need be, virtual coercion. Thus, his book, like any forward position, will be open to several ambushes by friends and foes alike.

Admitting a frank advocacy does not allow one to remain sheltered by a freedom-of-choice argument by which population planners have tried to avoid attacks by the opposition. Providing universal access to contraception seemed to imply that all population control meant was to help people do what they want—an aim generally viewed as laudatory, equivalent to free public education and equal access to health facilities. Frank advocacy of reducing fertility, and even planning some measures that may seem coercive, dispenses with the bland rhetoric about freedom of choice. Legislation that makes people forgo having children, even though they may want to have them, must be argued on different grounds—the overriding need to stabilize population, the primacy of important social needs over individual desires, and the clash between freedom to procreate and other individual rights such as privacy. Professor Barnett explores these arguments, stripping away some of the facades behind which population control advocates have been able to avoid controversies. He asks the challenging question: If we assume population control as a supreme value in policy, what are the legislative consequences?

The answers to this question may break up some of the coalitions in which population planning has been embedded. Although he is not the first to say so, Professor Barnett shows in detail how much current legislation, while admirable for other aims, favors increased fertility. Thus, legislative changes that would lead to a decrease in fertility would also counteract other aims that many people might hold dear. In this case people would have to make a choice between their belief in population control and other policy aims. One example of the conflict is welfare legislation for children. If one wants to discourage parents from having excessive numbers of children, an effective way would be for the state to stop subsidizing their upbringing. Accordingly, changes in the tax laws might be considered, including curtailment of personal exemptions for dependents or tuition charges in public schools. Population planners have frequently listened to the argument that these measures would punish innocent children for the antisocial behavior of their parents. This argument can make effective policies impossible, because there will always be some children already in existence when legislation is executed. Child welfare advocates who are also conscious of the danger of population increase will not be able to sidestep the conflict inherent in the two issues.

A similar conflict exists in the case of women's rights advocates. Feminists and population control advocates have generally supported each other; they agreed that contraception freed women from compulsory motherhood and that alternative careers for women were a necessary precondition for fertility decline. Professor Barnett shows how ambiguous is the evidence of a relationship between women's participation in the labor force and fertility decline and suggests that careers for women will reduce fertility only if the state does not enable women to have children while pursuing careers. Thus, child care, job sharing, and cooperative childrearing arrangements would have to be eliminated because they nullified the advantage for society (fertility decline) that arose from women's participation in the labor force. Society would have to decide whether other values relating to women's careers overrode the counterproductivity of subsidized child care as regards population control. Feminists, however, might view abolition of child care policies with a jaundiced eye.

Only some of the possible conflicts of serious population planners with erstwhile allies have been mentioned. These conflicts are examples of pronatalist policies deeply embedded in our legal structure. One might ask whether these policies are isolated instances or representatives of an underlying favoritism toward population increase. Such favoritism might have been productive in earlier periods of territorial expansion and may have become ingrained in our values, laws, and mores. In this case, not only adjustments in some laws, but a general reversal of policy backed by a major change in public opinion, will be needed if population growth has really become a menace.

One might object that increases in population will stop naturally since they cannot go on forever. Certainly the doomsday predictions found in the exercises of some demographers—such as the forecast that the population of the United States would reach the weight of the earth—will not come true. Nevertheless, some brakes will have to be applied, natural or not; it is questionable whether these brakes will be humane or pleasant. If no convenient world war or lethal epidemic intervenes as a natural brake, the social measures needed will be truly extreme policies, such as choices of victims of starvation, stringent licensing of childbearing, or other possibilities now found only in the more unpleasant volumes of science fiction. If we want to avoid these prospects, we have to look now for effective policies of population control. Professor Barnett has performed a signal service in assembling the areas of law that will be important to the role of the state in population control. As the start of an urgent discussion, this work can be read with profit by all concerned citizens.

KURT W. BACK

# PREFACE

A preface is a delightful device. It permits the author to cover a number of important points that do not easily fit into the body of the book, largely because they are of a personal nature. A preface thus allows the author to provide readers with insight into the roots of his undertaking.

My formal training has been both in law and in social science, but my principal intellectual commitment is to law. An attribute of law not shared by any science is that scholarship and advocacy are combined, the former being the foundation for the latter. Since it is legal in nature, the present book interweaves scholarship and advocacy, with a focus on population dynamics. I hope that the scholarship represented in this book will assist the reader in grasping some of the important legal concepts and principles relevant to population dynamics. The link between law and population has been seriously neglected, and I hope the book will promote interest in it. At the same time the book will, I hope, lead the reader to consider the position advocated—that the United States has reached its optimum population size, or probably even surpassed it by a substantial margin, if the conditions we deem essential to a high standard of living are to be preserved; and that a fertility control policy implemented through the legal system is both possible and necessary to halt population growth promptly. Continued increases in population numbers are causing serious problems, and, I submit, they necessitate the use of the only societal institution capable of rapidly and effectively inducing changes in individual conduct—namely, law. Nonetheless, I do not mean to suggest that the implementation of a fertility control policy will bring utopia. Fertility control will cause problems—particularly from the skewed age distribution that will follow a substantial reduction in births—but I believe the problems will be far less severe than those we will face without a prompt containment of domestic population numbers.

Several chapters in the book are based upon articles that I first published in legal journals, which have kindly granted permission for their reproduction. All of the articles, however, have been revised and incorporate additional materials. Chapter 2 stems from an article titled "Population Law: A Neglected Field" that appeared in volume 13 of the *Creighton Law Review* (1979). Chapter 3 is based on an article titled "Population Growth, Population Organization Participants, and the Right of Privacy" that was published in volume 12 of the *Family Law Quarterly* (1978). Chapter 4 stems from an article titled "Population Policy and Law in the United States," published in volume 3 of the *Harvard Journal of Law and Public Policy* (1980). Chapter 6 is a revision of an article, "Child Exclusion Policies in Housing," that first appeared in volume 67 of the *Kentucky Law Journal* (1978–79); copyright held by the *Kentucky Law Journal*.

This book is, I believe, the first in-depth examination of the interrelationship of population and law in the United States. The preparation of a book generates an intense awareness of the intellectual debt that the author owes to others, and this is true even in a new field, since a novel approach to a problem does not develop in a vacuum. Writing on the subject of population and law carries an especially large debt because it rests on contributions from many disciplines. Population law is necessarily a broadly based field, and its potential can be realized only to the extent that it draws from and builds upon other disciplines.

Two disciplines are particularly important to the field of population law. The first is biology. The implications of population numbers and growth cannot be fully understood without a familiarity with biology and its subfield ecology. The human species must be viewed as part of nature, on which its existence and quality of life literally depend. The size and activities of the human species have begun to affect nature seriously, but recognition of the impact requires a knowledge of biology. With this recognition, a wide variety of topics relevant to population law can be identified and the importance of the field to human welfare can be appreciated.

The second discipline that is important to population law is social science. The study of human population numbers has developed most rapidly within social science, particularly sociology, and social science accordingly possesses substantive information and research techniques that need to be understood in the field of population law. The reader will notice a large number of citations of social science research. Without this research, whatever contribution is made by the book would not have been possible.

Science exists only because of the people who have devoted themselves to it. The intellectual debt I owe the biological and social sciences is due to the many fine individuals in those fields with whom I have been fortunate to have had contact. Those who introduced me to population studies in the two fields deserve special tribute. Charles Nam taught me demography at Florida State University and first interested me in the population problem. His competence as a teacher is indicated by the fact that I started my study of demography with the assumption that the subject was dry and useless; indeed, I studied the subject only because I was under express orders from my Ph.D. committee to do so. Later, Paul Ehrlich introduced me to, and interested me in, the biological aspects of population, which led me to the works of other biologists. More than anyone else, these two individuals were responsible for my commitment to the study of population.

Scientific knowledge concerning population numbers and pressures is linked in this book to the legal system and particularly to its constitutional aspects. The link would not have been possible without the excellent education that I received at the University of Florida Law School. The years I spend there were exceptionally pleasant and proved that it is possible to enjoy being a student.

Among the law school faculty who influenced me, two people stand out. Fletcher Baldwin introduced me to constitutional law, a subject with which I have become utterly fascinated. Scott Van Alstyne and I spent many hours talking about the population problem. Both actively encouraged me to pursue my scholarly interests in law. Without their encouragement, I might not have done so.

This book has been a challenging and rewarding project, but the task of researching and writing the manuscript consumed a tremendous amount of time. The result was that my wife, Linda, was without a husband many evenings and weekends. Nonetheless, she has continued to be her gentle, good-natured self. Her support during this project—and, indeed, over the years—has been constant and her patience inexhaustible. Her role in allowing me to pursue my interest in the population problem cannot be overemphasized, and it is to her that this book is dedicated.

# I LEGAL DIMENSIONS OF THE POPULATION ISSUE

# 1 INTRODUCTION

This book is about a forgotten issue: the relationship between the legal system and increases in the number of Americans. Population size was a topic of considerable public concern in the period from 1969 to 1972, and during that time the legal aspects of population control attracted attention. Unfortunately, there has been no sustained interest in the legal implications of domestic population increase. However, it is very likely just a matter of time before the United States adopts a population policy — a policy in which law will play a central role. Population increase is not a major issue today, but the problem still exists and is not improving.

The decline of public interest in the population issue was evidently due in part to the belief that population growth in the United States had stopped or would soon do so.[1] The belief is mistaken. Population is increasing and will continue to mount unless the birth rate falls or the death rate rises. In 1950 we began the last half of the twentieth century with 151 million Americans; we began 1980 with 222 million.[2] If women now entering their childbearing years have an average of 2.1 children each — so-called replacement-level fertility — the population will rise by 26 million between 1980 and 2000 even without any net immigration, and numbers will continue to increase well into the next century. Indeed, twenty-one million people will be added between 2000 and 2040 before population size stabilizes.[3] Though this rate of growth is slower than the growth rates of developing nations, it is part of an increase in world population numbers that an international conference of legislators recently termed "staggering."[4] Population growth in the United States and elsewhere is intensifying the competition for, and raising the price of, resources Americans need to maintain their high standard of living. The international conference of legislators concluded: "At the global level, continuously expanding human demands have created intolerable pressures on resources, particularly energy. The pressures on biological resources—fisheries, forests, grasslands, and croplands—are mounting steadily and will continue to do so."[5]

## DEMOGRAPHIC SOURCES OF U.S. POPULATION GROWTH

Since the United States is not immune to population pressures on physical and biological resources, let us briefly examine the demographic sources of U.S. population growth. Natural increase—the excess of births over deaths—has been a more important source than net legal immigration. Since 1970 natural increase has totaled at least 1,163,000 annually, while immigration, according to official statistics, has never been higher than 449,000.[6] The substantial disparity between births and deaths is particularly inconsistent with the impression that the United States has reached, or is rapidly approaching, zero population growth. An important reason for the mistaken belief that the numbers of births and deaths are or will soon be equal lies in a misunderstanding of a demographic measure known as the *total fertility rate*. For example, in 1978 the rate was 1.80.[7] Many people wrongly interpreted this figure to mean that women were having an average of 1.8 children each. However, the total fertility rate for a given year represents the average number of children that women who are that year entering the age range for childbearing will have in their lifetimes if they experience the birth rates prevailing among women who are already in the age range for having children. The

INTRODUCTION 5

total fertility rate is thus a hypothetical measure because it is a projection of completed family size for women entering their childbearing period in a particular year, and it is based on the actual childbearing experience of all women who, in that year, are of an age to have children. Birth rates, however, vary from year to year and expose the "newcomers" to changing probabilities of having children as they pass through their childbearing period. Thus, actual completed family size usually differs significantly from what was projected by the total fertility rate.

Table 1.1 illustrates the hypothetical nature of the total fertility rate.[8] The table shows the rate prevailing in four years (1920, 1930, 1940, and 1948) and the average family size actually realized by women who finished their childbearing thirty years after each of these dates. The table thus provides an indication of the correspondence achieved between projected and actual family size. Of the four comparisons shown, a close correspondence existed between the total fertility rate and actual completed family size only once (1948/ 1978). Current projections are probably no more accurate. Indeed, women who were eighteen and nineteen years old in 1978 expected to have approximately 2.0 children each in their lifetimes, even though their total fertility rate was only about 1.8.[9]

The hypothetical nature of the total fertility rate is only part of the reason for the mistaken belief that natural increase is not continuing at a substantial level. Another factor is the age structure of the population. Replacement-level childbearing—that is, two children

Table 1.1. Hypothetical Nature of the Total Fertility Rate

| Year | Total Fertility Rate for Women Entering Childbearing Age | Year | Average Number of Children Previously Born to Women Presently 45-49 Years Old |
|---|---|---|---|
| 1920 | 3.26 | 1950 | 2.44 |
| 1930 | 2.53 | 1960 | 2.35 |
| 1940 | 2.23 | 1970 | 2.86 |
| 1948 | 3.03 | 1978 | 3.10 |

per couple—yields an equal number of births and deaths only when the different age groups in a population do not exhibit marked variations in size and when they only gradually diminish numerically as the result of attrition through deaths. When a given population contains a disproportionately large number of people in their childbearing years—as is the case in the United States because of the baby boom that followed World War II—two children do more than replace their parents.[10] Because young adults have a low death rate and remain in the population for several decades after having children, population growth results when young adults produce one child for each parent. An immediate halt to natural increase in the United States would require that the total fertility rate fall to slightly above 1.0 for some two decades.[11]

Natural increase is the most visible source of population growth, but immigration also plays an important role. The Bureau of the Census estimates that net legal immigration into the United States from 1970 to 1978 ranged from a yearly low of 315,000 to a high of 449,000.[12] These estimates, however, have been criticized for seriously understating the total flow of immigrants. Illegal immigration is believed to contribute a large number of people to the U.S. population annually, though the exact level is not known and estimates cover a wide range.[13]

U.S. population growth, in short, has been substantial during the seventies, and it probably will not diminish to any significant degree in the near future. It is within the context of this population increase that this book is written. The book is based on three premises. The first—that the United States has been experiencing serious problems because of population growth—is based on evidence found in chapters 2 and 3. The second premise is that, until an official fertility control policy is adopted, childbearing levels will be determined by factors that unintentionally influence people's motivation to have children. Some of these factors are discussed in chapters 4, 5, and 6. The third premise is that, because of the problems stemming from domestic population pressures, official measures to limit family size are necessary in the United States. Three possible measures are considered in chapters 7, 8, and 9. In addition, chapters 10 and 11 deal with two issues that have a bearing on population size and are presently the subject of considerable controversy: abortion and immigration.

The idea that formal fertility control measures are required in the United States is not widely accepted and is likely to encounter great resistance. The premise that government must intervene in order to influence the childbearing motivation of individuals is based on what has been labeled the "motivational" model of human nature. Among possible fertility control policies, the idea of government intervention is most likely to generate serious discord. It is not, however, a new idea.[14]

> The motivational approach assumes that, by and large, people will have children if they want them . . . that individuals desire children, and that policies would have to change this desire. Direct intervention with this desire becomes the only policy consistent with the model. From a societal point of view, this desire for children is connected with many structural and emotionally involved conditions. Hence, it becomes the politically most controversial policy, especially without an accompanying change in social conditions.[15]

## POPULATION GROWTH AND CONSTITUTIONAL LAW

The population issue can be viewed from many perspectives—economic, psychological, and sociological, for instance. This book uses law as its framework. The importance of a legal orientation rests on the fact that, although law has received insufficient attention in connection with the study of population, law is central to a consideration of public policy in any area. Law determines public policy through a variety of means—for example, statutes, regulations implementing statutes, and judicial determinations of the constitutionality of government action. This book emphasizes the constitutional dimension of public policy affecting population control. The constitutional factor is vital because the Constitution is the basic legal document of the nation; it both defines the subjects on which the federal government can act and establishes the limits of authority for all levels of government. The Constitution thus has two functions. First, it provides the federal government with its powers; federal action can extend only to issues explicitly or implicitly within its purview under the Constitution.[16] Second, the Constitution imposes constraints on the action of both federal and state governments in order to protect individuals and groups.[17] However, as an instrument "intended to endure for ages to come,"[18] the Constitution is a document of general provisions that must be applied to governmental action in concrete situations. The application of generally stated prescriptions to specific situations requires that the Constitution be interpreted by the judiciary, a process that reveals much about the important values of the political, economic, and social system of the United States.[19] In establishing the Constitution, the American people

> ... undertook to carry out for the indefinite future and in all the vicissitudes of the changing affairs of men, those fundamental purposes which the instrument itself discloses. Hence we read its words, not as we read legislative codes which are subject to continuous revision with the changing course of events, but as the revelation of the great purposes which were intended to be achieved by the Constitution as a continuing instrument of government.[20]

In examining the legal dimensions of the population issue, then, the principal focus of this book is on constitutional law because the Constitution as interpreted by the judiciary defines the nature of permissible government conduct affecting social structures and individual behavior and reflects the values of American society.

## NOTES

1. *See generally* Charles F. Westoff & James McCarthy, *Population Attitudes and Fertility,* 11 Family Planning Perspectives 93, 94 (1979).

2. Bureau of the Census, U.S. Department of Commerce, *Estimates of the Population of the United States and Components of Change: 1940 to 1978,* Current Population Reports, Series P-25, No. 802, at 8 (1979); Bureau of the Census, U.S. Department of Commerce, *Estimates of the Population of the United States to January 1, 1980,* Current Population Reports, Series P-25, No. 878 (1980).

3. Bureau of the Census, U.S. Department of Commerce, *Projections of the Population of the United States: 1977 to 2050,* Current Population Reports, Series P-25, No. 704, at 86 (1977).

4. Declaration of the International Conference of Parliamentarians on Population and Development (Colombo, Sri Lanka, 28 August-1 September 1979), *reprinted in*  5 Population & Development Review 730, 731 (1979). Legislators from fifty-eight countries, including the United States, participated in the conference.

5. *Id.*

6. Bureau of the Census, U.S. Department of Commerce, *Estimates of the*

*Population of the United States and Components of Change: 1940 to 1978,* Current Population Reports, Series P-25, No. 802, at 8 (1979).

7. *Id.* at 3.

8. National Center for Health Statistics, U.S. Department of Health, Education, & Welfare, Fertility Tables for Birth Cohorts by Color: United States, 1917-73 4, 124 (DHEW Pub. No. (HRA) 76-1152; Washington, D.C.: U.S. Gov't. Printing Office, 1976); Bureau of the Census, U.S. Department of Commerce, *Fertility of American Women: June 1978,* Current Population Reports, Series P-20, No. 341, at 32 (1979).

9. Bureau of the Census, *supra* note 8, at 10; Bureau of the Census, *supra* note 6, at 3.

10. Between 1970 and 1978, the number of Americans of childbearing age (i.e., 15 through 44 years old) increased from 85 million to 100 million. Americans 20 through 29 years old increased from 31 million to 38 million. Bureau of the Census, U.S. Department of Commerce, *Estimates of the Population of the United States by Age, Sex, and Race: 1976 and 1978,* Current Population Reports, Series P-25, No. 800, at 5, 6, 20 (1979).

11. Tomas Frejka, *Demographic Paths to a Stationary Population: The U.S. in International Comparison,* in Demographic and Social Aspects of Population Growth 623, 633 (Vol. I of the Research Reports of the U.S. Commission on Population Growth & the American Future, Charles F. Westoff & Robert Parke, Jr., eds.; Washington, D.C.: U.S. Gov't. Printing Office, 1972).

12. Bureau of the Census, *supra* note 6.

13. David Heer, *What is the Annual Net Flow of Undocumented Mexican Immigrants to the United States?* 16 Demography 417 (1979); J. G. Robinson, *Estimating the Approximate Size of the Illegal Alien Population in the United States by the Comparative Trend Analysis of Age-Specific Death Rates,* 17 Demography 159 (1980).

14. *E.g.,* David M. Heer, *Marketable Licenses for Babies: Boulding's Proposal Revisited,* 22 Social Biology 1 (1975).

15. Kurt W. Back & Nancy J. McGirr, *Population Policy and Models of Human Nature,* 2 Journal of Population 91, 97 (1979).

16. McCulloch v Maryland, 17 U.S. (4 Wheat.) 316, 405, 423 (1819).

17. *Id.* at 404, 423; Hurtado v California, 110 U.S. 516, 536 (1884).

18. McCulloch v Maryland, 17 U.S. (4 Wheat.) at 415.

19. The Constitution does not expressly authorize judicial review of the constitutionality of governmental action, but the Supreme Court inferred such authority from it in 1803. Marbury v Madison, 5 U.S. (1 Cranch) 137 (1803).

20. United States v Classic, 313 U.S. 299, 316 (1941).

# 2 POPULATION AND LAW

One of the most important changes that the American people are currently undergoing concerns assumptions about the world around them. These assumptions help constitute a mental map with which to perceive and deal with experience.[1] Traditionally, Americans have assumed that the human species could dominate nature, that their ability to change the world was unlimited, and that all problems were solvable. Experience is making these assumptions untenable, and new assumptions are gradually being adopted. The new assumptions emphasize that the human species is part of a complex community of many interdependent animal and plant species on the planet, that interdependence creates feedback within the community and sometimes results in unintended consequences flowing from a given action, and that change and growth have physical and biological limits. These assumptions, which stem from the branch of biological science known as ecology, encourage a recognition of the problems arising from the increase in human numbers, because increased population has created pressures on physical and biological resources. The science of ecology gave rise to these assumptions, which the American people are now beginning to accept, because they constitute an effective means to understand the world. As one observer has noted:

> [S]cience is a search for constancies, for invariants. It is the enterprise of making those identifications in experience which prove to be most significant for the control or appreciation of the experience yet to come. The basic scientific question is, "What the devil is going on around here?"[2]

While complete acceptance of the assumptions of ecology will necessarily be a slow if not painful process, there already appears to be considerable recognition that traditional assumptions about the human species and the limits of growth are obsolete. A national survey conducted in 1978 found that, for the first time since the question was posed in the late 1950s, Americans believed the future would be worse than the present and the past.[3] This attitude seems to be associated with people's acceptance of the new ecological assumptions. Another national survey done in 1978 found that a substantial number of people recognized the prospect, if not the current existence, of resource shortages.[4] Such a recognition inevitably leads to a focus on population growth.

## FAMILY PLANNING AND POPULATION SIZE

In the United States the pressures of human numbers on physical and biological resources necessarily involves the legal system, but the interrelationship between the population issue and law has received relatively little attention. The most frequently appearing scholarship relevant to the interrelationship concentrates on statutes, regulations, and court decisions concerning contraception, sterilization, and abortion—that is, the focus is on family planning. However, an important distinction must be made between family planning and the legal aspects of population size and growth. The family-planning perspective is concerned with the means by which an individual can control his or her fertility; family planning emphasizes freedom of choice in childbearing decisions and in the use of contraceptives and maximum access to safe, effective means of birth control, including abortion. Its principal emphasis is on the individual. The population perspective, on the other hand, examines the causes and consequences of the increase, decrease, and distribution of population numbers and thus places a heavier emphasis on large-scale, society-level phenomena.

The distinction between the two perspectives can be better understood if one examines the major assumptions on which each is based. The family-planning perspective makes the following assumptions:

1. Individuals should have absolute discretion to decide on the number of children they will have. Therefore, individuals should have ready access to contraception, sterilization, and abortion.
2. If population size must be limited, we can rely on individuals to curtail their childbearing in the best interests of society. Given easy access to safe, effective means of birth control and educated about the dangers of overpopulation, individuals will make voluntary childbearing decisions that will yield an appropriate population size. Accordingly, we need not be concerned with the welfare of society as long as we protect the welfare of the individual.

The population perspective, on the other hand, employs markedly different assumptions:

1. The causes and effects of changes in population numbers often differ from the causes and effects of individual decisions about childbearing. The former occur on a large scale, can be beyond the recognition and control of the individual, and have important ramifications for the nature and welfare of society.
2. The relationship between the causes and consequences of population numbers and actual change in population size is not necessarily linear in nature; change in the former may not be accompanied by a constant and consistent change in the latter.
   *a.* Any given cause of change in population numbers may intensify or abate but may not have much or any impact on actual population size until the causal factor reaches a certain threshold, at which point there may be a relatively

rapid change in numbers that is out of proportion to the degree of alteration in the cause.
   b. Changes in population numbers may not have much or any impact on social, economic, and ecological conditions until the numbers reach a certain threshold, at which point there may be a relatively large impact with a very small change in population size.
3. Motivation to limit family size is the most important factor in controlling population size. Population control requires more than the availability of contraception, sterilization, and abortion; it requires a personal commitment to limit family size.

## LAW AND THE POPULATION PERSPECTIVE

Let us examine some illustrations that arise from the assumption of the population perspective, which is new to the field of law. With regard to the first assumption about the causes of population growth, the legalization of contraception, sterilization, and abortion appears to reduce the birth rate.[5] Moreover, with a given level of access to birth control methods, substantial changes in childbearing levels may occur in response to other factors in the legal system. For instance, the baby boom that occurred after World War II may have resulted in part from the Internal Revenue Code's income tax exemption for children, which reduced the cost of childrearing.[6] With regard to the consequences of population growth, the birth of any one child will have an impact on the legal system so slight as to be unmeasurable, but (as argued in chapter 3) the birth of a large number of children will result in a level of population growth that may reduce the protections afforded by the constitutional right of privacy.

With regard to the second assumption on which the population perspective is based, research providing clear illustrations is lacking because such illustrations require sophisticated, quantitative research to identify the nature of the relationship between population size on the one hand and its causes and consequences on the other. One possible illustration with respect to the causes of population growth might be the child-exclusion policies adopted by some apartments and condominiums. Such policies will have little effect on fertility when they are confined to a small proportion of the housing units in a given area but will have an important effect as soon as the policies are sufficiently prevalent to create housing shortages for parents. Whether child-exclusion policies are permitted by statute and court decision affects their prevalence.[7] Another possibility with respect to the causes of population growth is that child care facilities for employed women may promote childbearing, but that the facilities' impact on the birth rate occurs only after they reach a certain level of prevalence in a given geographic region.[8] The availability of child care facilities will be determined partly by the existence or absence of governmental incentives; the number of child care facilities was undoubtedly increased by a change in the Internal Revenue Code that permitted employers making capital expenditures for such facilities for the children of their employees to deduct the expenditures in calculating their federal income tax.[9] With regard to the consequences of population growth, a possible illustration may be found in the increases since 1950 in the number of people who are awake and active during the night. Increased nighttime activity has an influence on the operation of the legal system and particularly on law enforcement.[10] Since the increase seems to have started at a certain point in time, it may have resulted from a critical threshold having been exceeded by population numbers.

The third assumption of the population perspective emphasizes that the causes of different fertility levels are to be found primarily in the motivation to use birth control methods rather than in the accessibility of such technology, which is in widespread and effective use in the United States today.[11] That is, the number of births will be most effectively controlled when people capable of having children *want* to limit their fertility.[12] An illustration from the field of law, though not from the United States, is found in the stringent population control policy currently being implemented in the People's Republic of China. With the aim of ending natural increase by the end of the century, the central government is adopting legislation creating economic rewards for couples having no more than one child and economic penalties for couples having more than two.[13] China has thus recognized that curtailment of population growth requires strong incentives incorporated into its legal system.

The assumption that motivation is most important in limiting family size raises the issue of coercion in population control because it focuses attention on incentives to limit childbearing. If individuals are encouraged to have a certain number of children by a system of rewards and penalties, have they not lost their freedom to determine the size of their families? One of the most articulate spokesmen for the population perspective has labeled the controversy over "compulsory" versus "voluntary" measures a false issue because it overlooks the fact that reproductive decisions are always the result of the social, economic, and cultural setting in which people live:

> To say that couples should have exactly the number of children they want, taken by itself, is an anarchic slogan. It says nothing about how people's desires in this regard are determined. The desire for [a certain number of] children is not a pure accident. It is not biologically determined. It is engendered by social and economic circumstances. If I want four children but feel that my economic circumstances make only two advisable, then I am involuntarily constrained by economic circumstances. An exclusively family-planning approach to fertility limitation *assumes* that what individuals want is identical with what society needs; it therefore sees no need to change social institutions so as to influence reproductive motivation. It therefore can say that its approach is "voluntary" and that other approaches are "compulsory." A program [of population control], however, would be more realistic in endeavoring to change reproductive motivation by making it to the individual's *interest* to reproduce less.[14]

The motivation to have a certain number of children, in short, is the result of incentives. The incentives may be official or unofficial, intentional or unintentional, legal or sociological. Whatever their nature, they exist in every society, and the population perspective focuses on them.

The population perspective has not been applied extensively to the field of law in the United States. Considerably more attention has been given to the population perspective in the legal systems of developing countries, but even in these countries the study of the interrelationship of population and law is just beginning.[15] Nonetheless, the progress made to date has led one Asian legal scholar to write:

> The evolution of "Population Law" is undoubtedly the most innovative and socially relevant development that has taken place in the sphere of law in recent times. . . . Lawyers have become sensitized to social problems which

affect the quality of life both at the micro-level of the family unit and at the macro-level of the community or nation. Social scientists have identified a new input to be built into population and development programmes.[16]

## LEGISLATION STEMMING FROM POPULATION GROWTH

The remainder of this chapter focuses on one aspect of population law: recent legislation enacted by Congress that has resulted in large measure from population growth in the United States. The chapter provides illustrations of the consequences of population growth under the first assumption of the population perspective. The illustrations are particularly useful because legislation is normally not enacted unless a certain subject is considered a serious problem. Accordingly, the illustrations can help identify some of the areas where the impact of population pressures is particularly severe.

In selecting the legislation that would be included, a number of criteria were employed. First, population pressures must have been an obvious cause of the problem with which the legislation dealt or must have been shown by research to constitute a cause. Second, the problem must have stemmed from population growth in the United States, not from population growth elsewhere. Third, the legislation had to be of substantial importance in and of itself; brief amendments and legislation appropriating funds for already existing programs were not included. Fourth, the legislation must have been enacted in the years 1971 through 1978[17] — a recent period sufficiently long to permit the identification of the major problems caused by domestic population growth. Legislation that met these criteria was organized into four general categories: environment and natural resources, the economy, built surroundings, and health.

### Laws Affecting the Environment and Natural Resources

Probably the most serious effects of population pressures are found in the quality of the natural environment and in the availability of natural resources. The standard of living of any society is dependent on the ecosystems in its geographic area and on the resources, both physical and biological, provided by its environment. To the extent that ecosystems do not function smoothly and resources are not adequate, the quality of life of a society is diminished. The natural environment and its resources are thus the foundation upon which human societies are built, and they are subject to population-induced problems.

*Land.* Three problems involving land have been covered by recent legislation. The first was soil conservation. Congress enacted the Soil and Water Resource Conservation Act of 1977 in order to develop (1) information on the quality, quantity, and use of soil, water, and related resources (e.g., fish and wildlife habitats) and (2) a national program of soil and water conservation.[18] The act resulted from a finding that pressures on soil and water resources were substantial and increasing. The report on the bill by the House of Representatives identified the role of domestic population numbers in creating the need for legislation:

> Among the ever-increasing pressures caused by population growth are greater demands on soil, water, and related resources in order to meet both present and future requirements for food and fiber; for rural and urban development; for agricultural, industrial, and community water supplies; for fish and wildlife habitats; and for an untold variety of other needs and uses.[19]

Because the United States is by far the leading source of grain for the world market,[20] the impact of population growth on domestic agricultural land is of considerable importance both to the nation and to the world. By possessing and controlling grain exports, the United States can influence the policies of foreign governments, reduce the deficit in its balance of payments in international trade, and promote at least short-term humanitarian goals. The impact of population numbers on agricultural land occurs in at least two ways. First, population expansion forces the conversion of agricultural land to nonagricultural uses—for example, housing, reservoirs, and roads. Approximately 3 million acres of farmland, including 1 million acres of prime farmland, are lost to other uses each year. Each decade, therefore, roughly 7 percent of all agricultural land and 4 percent of prime lands are converted to nonagricultural uses.[21] Second, population growth promotes soil erosion from wind and water. As population numbers increase, agricultural land is used more intensively for food production, marginal land is brought into production, and forests are cut to acquire lumber for buildings and to increase the amount of food-producing land. Soil erosion on such land is greater than on land that is used little or not at all.[22] The seriousness of erosion in the United States is indicated by the fact that one-third of the topsoil on croplands has been lost over the past two hundred years, a loss that includes some 100 million acres of cropland that since 1935 has deteriorated to the point where it can no longer be cultivated.[23] (The loss of 100 million acres is equivalent to losing the area covered by the state of California.)[24] The United States today has a total of only some 400 million acres of cropland and has limited ability to replace lost cropland with land not currently devoted to agriculture.[25]

A second problem with which federal legislation dealt was the deterioration of rangelands. The Forest and Rangeland Renewable Resources Research Act of 1978 authorized support for research on the protection, management, and utilization of forests and rangelands and for dissemination of the resulting information.[26] The Public Rangelands Improvement Act of 1978 provided a program to develop, inventory, manage, and improve publicly owned rangelands.[27] One study leading to passage of the law found that, of 163 million acres of public rangelands, 83 percent were in no better than "fair" condition. In addition, four of every six acres were not improving in quality, and one of every six acres was declining in quality, primarily because of unregulated grazing.[28] The number of grazing livestock is partially a function of the size of the human population that needs to be supported; as population numbers rise, the number of livestock will also tend to increase. As livestock numbers mount, overgrazing becomes a greater threat, and serious ecological problems can result—for example, soil erosion, flooding, creation of deserts, and water of reduced quality and quantity for human consumption, agriculture, and fish production.[29] Therefore, an increase in population numbers, which leads to increased grazing, requires that the use of rangelands be regulated and the number of livestock limited. This limitation may, in turn, have effects that many people will deem undesirable—for example, a reduction in the meat available for consumption.

The third piece of legislation involving land concerned forests. In addition to the Forest and Rangeland Renewable Resources Research Act of 1978 already mentioned, Congress enacted the National Forest Management Act of 1976, which requires the development of plans to manage the national forest system.[30] Lumber from the system accounts for a substantial proportion of the annual harvest of timber in the United States and has an important influence on the price paid for timber by the American public.[31] All else being equal, the demand for lumber (particularly in housing) increases with population size, and thus population growth places greater pressures on the productivity of forests, public and private. There is evidence that forest yields will not increase, and may even decline, in the next few decades, or that forest resources will be reduced if yields are increased.[32] The result will be a reduction in the per capita availability of timber and higher prices for timber either in the short term or in the long term. The demand for lumber will thus come into conflict with the vital ecological role played by forests, which act to minimize erosion and the buildup of sediment in rivers and reservoirs, to prevent water runoff and flooding, and to facilitate the global cycling of water, oxygen, carbon, and nitrogen.[33]

*Water.* Congress has enacted legislation concerned with both the quality and the quantity of water. With regard to quality, three laws have been passed to reduce water pollution.[34] The scale of such pollution is clearly enormous. It has been estimated that the abatement of water pollution under existing legislation will require the expenditure of $84 billion by public agencies and $76 billion by private organizations between 1979 and 1988.[35] Population growth plays a role in generating such pollution. Other things being equal, an increase in population numbers results in increased pollution from (1) greater use of rivers, lakes, and other bodies of water to dispose of the waste generated by increasing numbers of humans and livestock, (2) the chemicals discharged by more extensive industrial activity, and (3) the fertilizers, pesticides, and herbicides washed off land being farmed more intensively.[36] The fact that the number of Americans increased by 18 million in the 1970s[37] helps explain the lack of significant progress, despite federal legislative efforts, in water pollution abatement during that decade.[38]

With regard to the quantity of water available, three statutes have been enacted in an attempt to increase domestic water supplies.[39] In addition, a bill was passed for the control or reduction of salt levels in the water of the Colorado River Basin in order to increase supplies for individuals, industry, and agriculture; water treatment was required because human use was adding to a relatively high salt level that existed naturally.[40]

Continued population growth is largely responsible for a constantly increasing demand for water for personal consumption, industry, and agriculture. Americans use great amounts of water to maintain their high standard of living. Approximately 3,750 gallons of water per capita are used daily to provide food for each individual, and an additional 1,800 gallons per capita are used for industry, personal consumption, and other purposes.[41] Use of water—and, consequently, our standard of living—will apparently have to be reduced if population growth persists. Evidence indicates that, in spite of legislation, serious water shortages will exist in many regions of the United States in the near future.

> In summary, then, growth in population and economic activities during the next half century will force upon us significant expenditures for [water] treatment and storage facilities; moreover, for a growing number of regions, such investments will eventually prove inadequate. When one takes a region-by-region look at the situation, it becomes clear that the scope for redistribution of water, activities, and people is more limited and difficult to achieve than it might appear at first glance. But there is considerable scope for inducing reductions in demand for water. Short of significant technological breakthroughs in water augmenting procedures, this is the method that will have to be relied upon to hold expenditures on treatment and storage facilities to reasonable levels and to avoid difficult and painful redistributions. Population growth has a large role to play in determining how rapidly we must accomplish all these changes.[42]

*Wildlife.* Congress has enacted three laws dealing with animal and plant species that are or could be seriously jeopardized in the absence of regulation. The Fish and Wildlife Improvement Act of 1978 authorizes funds for research on, and resource management (including land acquisition) to protect, fish and wildlife.[43] The Endangered Species Act of 1973 provides programs to propagate threatened plant and animal species and to protect the ecosystems upon which such species depend.[44] Moreover, legislation has been passed to halt the decline in the number of wild, free-roaming horses and burros on public lands—a decline due to human misuse of the animals.[45]

The threat to animal species is a serious worldwide problem. Over half of the animal species known to have become extinct have disappeared in the present century, and an estimated one species or subspecies becomes extinct each year; in the United States, over 100 species of birds and mammals are considered to be in jeopardy at this time.[46] The potential repercussions for human welfare are serious because each species occupies a niche in an ecosystem, and the disappearance of a species leaves a gap that can disrupt the functioning of the entire ecosystem. Crop loss and the spread of disease can result.[47] Population growth and its correlates play a major, if not the key, role in the disappearance of species. The destruction of habitats appears to be the major factor in extinctions occurring in recent times; as population numbers have mounted, construction of housing, roads, dams, and recreational facilities has spread. More extensive farming and logging has also intruded upon previously undisturbed areas. In addition to altering habitats, rising population numbers have fostered increased use of pesticides and herbicides in agriculture and of chemicals and metals in industry; the result has been the pollution of water needed by wildlife. Extinction has always taken place in nature, but the increasing scale of human activity has accelerated the process and has totally obliterated some genetic strains. The Council on Environmental Quality notes that "[m]an depends directly on thousands of species of living organisms for his needs, and indirectly on the adaptive diversity and ecological roles played by countless others."[48] Population growth is eroding this indispensable basis for human existence.

*Coastal Zone and Oceans.* Several pieces of legislation have been enacted to deal with coastal land and ocean waters and their resources. The Coastal Zone Management Act of 1972 calls for the preparation and implementation of state plans and management programs to protect the coastal zone.[49] The Marine Mammal Protection Act of 1972 requires U.S. citizens to obtain a permit to take marine mammals, including whales, porpoises, seals, and sea otters.[50]

The Marine Protection, Research, and Sanctuaries Act of 1972 regulates the dumping into the ocean of waste that originated in the United States or that originated elsewhere but is to be deposited in American-controlled ocean waters.[51] The Deepwater Port Act of 1974 authorizes the construction and operation of ports located in deep waters beyond the territorial limits of the United States for the use of large oil tankers.[52] The Ports and Waterways Safety Act of 1972 is aimed at the prevention of pollution caused by damage to structures and vessels in navigable waters.[53]

The need for all of this legislation can be traced in large measure to population growth. Increased numbers of people result in greater residential, recreational, and industrial development and more fishing and mineral extraction in coastal areas, and in increased use of the ocean for dumping and transportation. Thus, for example, shellfish in coastal waters appear to be experiencing increased contamination from metals and chemicals and to be declining in quantity.[54] The overall result is degradation of the natural environment and intensified exploitation of its resources. In the words of Congress:

> The increasing and competing demands upon the lands and waters of our coastal zone occasioned by population growth and economic development, including requirements for industry, commerce, residential development, recreation, extraction of mineral resources and fossil fuels, transportation and navigation, waste disposal, and harvesting of fish, shellfish, and other living marine resources, have resulted in the loss of living marine resources, wildlife, [and] nutrient-rich areas, permanent and adverse changes to ecological systems, decreasing open space for public use, and shoreline erosion.[55]

*Mineral Resources and Energy.* The United States is entering an era of serious shortages of minerals, including minerals used to produce energy. The resource abundance of the past, particularly of the quarter-century following World War II, is coming to an end, and the inflation and unemployment that have characterized the economy since the early 1970s are manifestations of the growing imbalance between supply and demand.[56] The high U.S. standard of living has been based largely on the country's high per capita use of mineral resources, but Americans are gradually beginning to realize that mineral consumption is based to a very considerable extent on imported commodities. Of thirty-seven minerals important to the American economy for instance, at least half of the total consumption of twenty-two of them was imported in 1975.[57] Heavy dependence on foreign sources of vital minerals has become particularly serious because worldwide competition for minerals is rapidly intensifying as developing countries with large and growing populations attempt to industrialize.[58] In a 1975 report, the National Academy of Sciences predicted that "man faces the prospect of a series of shocks of varying severity as shortages occur in one material after another, with the first real shortages perhaps only a matter of a few years away."[59] Congress has also recognized the seriousness of the situation. In 1974 congressional legislation created a temporary National Commission on Supplies and Shortages to acquire information on the prospects for shortages and their causes and consequences.[60] In 1976, Congress passed the Solid Waste Disposal Act to promote the recovery of energy and other resources from discarded materials;[61] an express motivation for the legislation was concern over domestic shortages of minerals.[62]

While the United States faces shortages of a wide array of minerals important to its affluence,[63] Congress has most clearly recognized the problem of shortages in energy resources. Considerable legislation has been enacted to promote both the conservation and the production of energy.[64] "The fundamental reality," said one congressional committee, "is that this nation has entered a new era in which energy resources previously abundant will remain in short supply, retarding our economic growth and necessitating an alteration in our life's habits and expectations."[65]

Unfortunately, the role of population growth in creating and exacerbating the energy shortage has not been appreciated. Total energy consumption is the result of two distinct factors: number of people and per capita consumption. Multiplication of these factors yields total consumption. The size of the population affects the first factor in an obvious manner, but it also affects per capita consumption. With increases in population size, per capita consumption is forced up, as illustrated by the following two situations. Traffic jams occur when more vehicles use a road than the road can optimally accommodate. Each vehicle encounters difficulty in moving, and thus its energy consumption rises. Again, in the case of procurement of natural resources such as minerals, the minerals highest in grade and geographically closest are exploited more rapidly than they would otherwise be as a result of population growth. As nearby resources are exhausted, increased energy must be used to acquire less accessible resources to supply the needs of each member of the population.[66] Population growth creates, in short, diseconomies of scale. Thus, it is no accident that the proportion of a population employed by government increases both with the concentration of people and, after an optimum level is reached, with their number; government is forced to deal with problems of coordination and control that result from, and develop more rapidly than, the increase in population size.[67] The additional resources consumed to maintain political and social equilibrium necessarily raise a society's per capita energy consumption.

*Natural Disasters and Weather.* Congress has enacted several pieces of legislation dealing with natural disasters, particularly disasters caused by weather. The consequences of natural disasters increase with population numbers because injuries, deaths, and property damage from severe weather and other adverse acts of nature increase as the population in disaster-stricken areas rises. Since 1973 Congress has passed four bills aimed at alleviating the effects of natural disasters and attempting to deal with their causes.[68] Thus, Congress enacted legislation to develop a national policy on weather modification and a national program for research on the subject in order to find means to avert severe storms, drought, hurricanes, and tornadoes.[69] It also enacted the National Climate Program Act, whose aim is the advancement of knowledge of the causes and consequences of climatic change.[70] In adopting the act, Congress noted that "[w]eather and climate change affect food production, energy use, land use, water resources and other factors vital to national security and human welfare"[71]—consequences whose scale increases as population size mounts. Finally, Congress passed the Earthquake Hazards Reduction Act of 1977 in order to minimize risks to life and property from earthquakes.[72] An important reason for the law was the recognition that "[e]arthquakes have caused, and can cause in the future, enormous loss of life, injury, destruction of property, and economic and social disruption"[73]—effects that are magnified with increases in population numbers in stricken areas.

## Laws Affecting the Economy

An argument sometimes advanced with vigor is that population growth is necessary for economic progress.[74] The argument apparently stems partly from a misunderstanding of the writings of the major economic theorist of the twentieth century, John Maynard Keynes, who in fact believed that population stability can promote economic welfare.[75] Fortunately, the American public generally seems not to accept the argument that economic prosperity is dependent upon population growth; a 1971 national survey found that slightly over half of those interviewed rejected the argument.[76] However, rejection of the argument does not mean that Americans are cognizant of the negative consequences of population expansion; on the contrary, it appears that a clear recognition of the economic costs of continued population growth is still lacking. Accordingly, we need to examine some legislation dealing with economic problems that have resulted to a significant degree from domestic population pressures.

*Employment.* Several laws have been enacted aimed at reducing the number of unemployed persons,[77] but perhaps the most significant was the Full Employment and Balanced Growth Act of 1978, a commitment on the part of the federal government to attempt simultaneously to alleviate unemployment and to balance the budget, minimize inflation, improve the balance of trade with foreign nations, and achieve gains in productivity.[78] Special attention was given to the relatively high rate of unemployment among young adults; the act declared that "serious unemployment and economic disadvantage of a unique nature exist among youths, even under generally favorable conditions."[79] Congress found that federal monetary and fiscal policies had failed to attain previously established goals and that the policies must be supplemented by other measures.

The problem of unemployment can be largely explained by existing population pressures. The number of workers has been expanding rapidly in recent years as the result of the baby boom following World War II. For example, the number of young adults eighteen to twenty-four years old increased from roughly 16 million in 1960 to 29 million in 1979 — an 80 percent increase in just nineteen years.[80] The economy has been unable to absorb the rapid increase in the number of young workers produced by the baby boom; therefore, in the last few years about half of all unemployed persons have been twenty-four years of age or younger.[81] The unemployment problem today is to a considerable degree the result of the high fertility of the late 1940s and the 1950s.

Another law reflecting population pressures is the Federal Employees Flexible and Compressed Work Schedules Act of 1978, which authorized a three-year experiment in varying the length of the workweek and workday of federal government employees.[82] Rather than work five days a week and eight hours each day, employees were given the option of working, for example, ten hours a day for four days. Changes in the standard weekly work schedule of five eight-hour days have also begun in nongovernmental employment and have been motivated in part by the pressures that population numbers have placed on urban transportation systems at certain times of the day. Flexibility in work schedules can spread the use of streets, freeways, and mass transit over a longer period of time and thus reduce the congestion of "rush hours."[83]

*Taxation and Government Revenues.* In determining taxable income, the Internal Revenue Code permits taxpayers to deduct from their income a fixed amount for each dependent child. Until 1978 the amount was $750 for each child, but it was increased to $1,000 commencing in January 1979.[84] Congress gave the following reason for the change:

> The $750 exemption became effective in 1972. Inflation since then has eroded the real value of the $750 exemption and increased the difference between $750 and the cost of supporting a dependent. Consumer prices have in fact increased 55 percent since 1972. This erosion in the value of the exemption has been particularly severe for middle- and upper-middle-income taxpayers, especially those with large families.[85]

The inflation the United States has experienced since 1972 can be explained in large measure by population pressures, particularly as they have affected oil supplies and prices.[86] It is therefore ironic that congressional motivation for the increased exemption was the impact of inflation on large families, because financial relief was provided to the very people who have helped to foster inflation.

Population numbers appear to have reached the point where they are pressing against the limits to growth, and the pressures are manifested in shortages and concomitant price increases.[87]

In addition to reducing federal revenues to provide assistance to large families, Congress in 1972 authorized the transfer of federal revenues to state and local governments to defray their operating expenses and capital expenditures.[88] State and local governments, Congress found, were carrying the principal burden of domestic problems and were experiencing a rapid rise in the need for their services. Congress concluded that the increased demand for services stemmed largely from the growth of population numbers in general and growth in urban areas in particular.[89] Thus, it can be argued that Congress was subsidizing childbearing and population growth through tax law changes that reduced revenues, while at the same time it was spending revenues to alleviate the problems generated by population growth.

## Laws Affecting Built Surroundings

Federal legislation relevant to man-made physical surroundings can be divided into two categories: cities and housing.

*Cities.* Congress has enacted a number of laws dealing with the quality of life in urban areas. The National Neighborhood Policy Act established a commission to identify and make recommendations to alleviate the factors reducing the quality of life in urban neighborhoods;[90] the law followed a congressional finding that incentives needed to preserve the built environment were lacking and that deterioration would continue until explicit incentives were developed to encourage conservation of existing neighborhoods.[91] The Livable Cities Act of 1978 provided assistance to state and local governments and to private organizations for programs promoting the aesthetic and psychological aspects of urban areas, particularly for low- and moderate-income residents.[92] The Urban Park and Recreation Recovery Act of 1978 authorized assistance for recreational facilities in low-income urban neighborhoods.[93] Finally, the Solid Waste Disposal Act was directed at the recovery of energy and other resources from discarded materials and at the safe disposal of such materials.[94] The act was a response to the need to deal with the tremendous volume of waste generated by the population; waste has, in fact, begun to exceed the capacity of disposal sites available to urban areas.[95]

As urban popultions grow larger as a consequence of population increase in the nation as a whole, the quality of urban life tends to decline. The decline is manifested in the suburbanization process that has been occurring over the past half-century; many Americans seem to have concluded that areas of high population density are less attractive than areas of low density, and the difference they perceive in the quality of life has motivated them to live in low-density areas.[96] In the words of a computer simulation study of the dynamics of urban areas:

> Other things being equal, an increase in population of a city crowds housing, overloads job opportunities, causes congestion, increases pollution, encourages crime, and reduces almost every component of the quality of life.[97]

*Housing.* Congress has passed legislation to facilitate the purchase and ownership of housing. The Emergency Home Purchase Assistance Act of 1974 increased the availability of funds for mortgages in order to counteract shortages of, and high interest rates on, such funds.[98] The Emergency Housing Act of 1975 authorized temporary assistance with mortgage payments for persons unemployed or underemployed because of the economic recession that then existed.[99] One catalyst for housing legislation was the reduction in employment and capital stemming from shortages of energy and from rapid increases in the cost of energy.[100] Other problems involving housing added to the need for the legislation. For example, since the late 1960s the cost of purchasing housing has risen faster than income.[101] The high cost has been principally due to shortages of land.[102] During the same period the operating costs of housing have also advanced more rapidly than income, largely because of the increased price of heat and utilities.[103] It can be argued that population growth not only helped to create the shortages of land, capital, and energy that retarded income and raised housing costs; it also caused environmental degradation leading to governmental regulation that further contributed to housing expenses.[104]

### Laws Affecting Health

Congressional legislation dealing with health can be divided into two categories: (1) food and nutrition and (2) environmental insults.

*Food and Nutrition.* It is not widely appreciated that population growth in the United States has contributed to nutritional problems among American citizens. The National Agricultural Research, Extension, and Teaching Policy Act of 1977 was enacted to advance domestic food production through increased research and dissemination of information,[105] but while lawmakers recognized that population growth had helped to create the need for the law, they emphasized increased food production in order to provide for a larger population in the future.[106] Currently existing nutritional deficiencies led Congress to act, but neither of the two pieces of legislation that resulted recognized the role of past or current population growth in creating the deficiencies. Congress first passed the Food Stamp Act of 1977, which amended previous legislation to upgrade the nutrition of the poor.[107] The act made food stamps available to households whose financial resources were "a substantially limiting factor" to adequate nutrition.[108] Additional legislation promoted the nutrition of children in limited-income families[109] and the nutrition of low-income mothers both during pregnancy and up to one year after they had given birth.[110] The premise underlying each piece of legislation was that financial limitations were responsible for inadequate nutrition. The role of population growth in creating the financial limitations was ignored. However, population growth appears to have (1) forced food prices to rise and thereby made it more difficult for low-income persons to obtain an adequate diet and (2) held down incomes.

Let us examine the means by which population growth seems to foster financial limitations that affect nutrition. Population growth tends to increase food prices in the following ways:[111]

- Soil erosion and the use of marginal lands for agriculture are promoted. Yields on eroded and marginal lands are less than on high-quality land unless there is a greater investment of energy

(for example, in the form of fertilizer). Greater use of energy increases the cost of the food produced.
- Shortages of energy are created and the price of energy increased. Modern agriculture uses large amounts of energy for producing, processing, and transporting food, which makes the cost of food highly sensitive to the cost of energy.
- Capital becomes scarce and its price rises (as reflected in interest rates). Thus, the cost of agricultural equipment, energy, and land — and hence the cost of food — is forced up.
- Agricultural land must be converted to urban uses — for example, housing and transportation; as a result, the supply of agricultural land is reduced and its price increased, which affects food costs.

Population growth also appears to promote inequalities in income and hence to limit purchasing power among low-income groups. On the one hand, population growth increases the quantity of young workers. Recent studies have found that, because of their increasing numbers, young adults entering the labor force in the mid-1970s experienced a greater disparity than those entering in the late 1960s between the income they were able to earn and the income earned by older, already established workers. In other words, in response to the greater supply of young adults, the earnings of new entrants into the labor market fell further behind the earnings of their elders.[112] Increasing population numbers have thus contributed to the greater incidence of low incomes that prevail among young adults.[113]

On the other hand, population growth appears also to have an effect on workers' skills. There is evidence that high fertility causes less parental time and fewer financial resources to be devoted to each child and affects children's educational attainment. High fertility also results in lower expenditures per capita for public education. Large families thus seem to reduce the quality and hence the earning ability of the labor force by inhibiting the acquisition of skills.[114]

*Environmental Insults.* Environmental insults refer to man-made stimuli that have a deleterious effect on physical and mental health. As the population grows larger, these stimuli either increase in intensity or, because of the larger number of people exposed to them, increase in importance. Congress has enacted legislation authorizing research and education regarding the effects of noise. It has also set noise emission standards for newly made products that are major sources of noise.[115] Noise has been found to damage both physical and mental health[116] and to become more intense as population size expands.[117]

In another effort to deal with harmful stimuli, Congress passed the Federal Environmental Pesticide Control Act of 1972 to regulate the use of pesticides.[118] Even though pesticides are a potential threat to health, they cannot be completely banned because of the essential role they play in promoting agricultural productivity and minimizing food prices for our large and growing population.[119] Also, the National Cancer Act of 1971 was enacted in an attempt to facilitate research on and treatment of cancer.[120] Researchers believe most cancers to be the product of environmental causes,[121] and as population size increases in an industrial society, the prevalence of toxic elements in the environment, and the number of people exposed to them, can be expected to mount also.

Congress has also adopted legislation to help deal with child abuse and neglect and with the rising incidence of children who have run away from home.[122] Research indicates that children in crowded housing are more likely than other children to experience situations associated with abuse and running away.[123] Continued population growth raises the probability of crowded housing.[124]


Population increase in the United States has been an important cause of a variety of serious problems, and it cannot continue to be viewed with equanimity. The American people must recognize that population growth is eroding their standard of living—indeed, our environment may not be able to sustain our present standard of living even if population numbers remain at their present level.[125] We are paying a definite price for our failure to adopt a policy regulating family size. It may be that Americans will choose to sacrifice a high standard of living in order to avoid a fertility control policy, but we ought to be aware of the choice we are making.

## NOTES

1. S. I. Hayakawa, Language in Thought and Action, 2d ed., 30-32 (New York: Harcourt, Brace & World, 1964). An illustration of a mental map or identification system that permits human experience to be organized and controlled both in everyday life and in science is that of the Western formulation of time. An unsuccessful attempt to change the Western temporal framework occurred in France between 1793 and 1805; the failure resulted in part from the change required in the mental map of French citizens. Eviatar Zerubavel, *The French Republican Calendar: A Case Study in the Sociology of Time,* 42 American Sociological Review 868 (1977).

2. Abraham Kaplan, The Conduct of Inquiry 85 (San Francisco: Chandler, 1964).

3. Albert H. Cantril & Susan Cantril, Unemployment, Government and the American People 16 (Washington, D.C.: Public Research, 1978).

4. Opinion Research Corporation, XXXVI ORC Public Opinion Index 2-7 (September 1978); Riley E. Dunlap & Kent Van Liere, "Commitment to the Dominant Social Paradigm and Support for Ecological Policies: An Empirical Analysis" (revision of paper presented at the 1978 meeting of the Society for the Study of Social Problems).

5. *See* Karl Bauman, Ann Anderson, J. L. Freeman, & G. Koch, *Legal Abortions, Subsidized Family Planning Services, and the U.S. "Birth Dearth,"* 24 Social Biology 183 (1977). In finding that government funding of already legal contraceptive services does not reduce the birth rate but that the legalization of abortion may do so, the study suggests that the important factor is the legality of birth control.

6. Peter H. Lindert, Fertility and Scarcity in America 134-35, 170 (Princeton, N.J.: Princeton University Press, 1978).

7. *See* chapter 6, *infra.*

8. Josefina Card, *The Malleability of Fertility-Related Attitudes and Behavior in a Filipino Migrant Sample,* 15 Demography 459, 475 (1978).

9. I.R.C. § 188. The change permitted deductions for expenditures made beginning January 1, 1972. The Select Committee on Population of the House of Representatives, which existed in 1978, recommended that Congress consider the expansion of financial support for child care facilities. House Select Committee on Population, *Final Report,* 95th Cong., 2d Sess. 44, 51 (1978).

10. Murray Melbin, *Night as Frontier,* 43 American Sociological Review 3, 4, 9-12 (1978).

11. Kathleen Ford, *Contraceptive Use in the United States, 1973-1976,* 10 Family Planning Perspectives 264 (1978); Charles Westoff, *The Decline in Unwanted Fertility, 1971-1976,* 13 Family Planning Perspectives 70 (1981).

12. Judith Blake & P. Gupta, *Reproductive Motivation versus Contraceptive Technology: Is Recent American Experience an Exception?* 1 Population & Development Review 229 (1975).

13. Chen Muhua, *Birth Planning in China,* 11 Family Planning Perspectives 348 (1979).
14. *World Population: A Global Perspective: Hearings Before the Select Committee on Population,* 95th Cong., 2d Sess. 516, 521 (1978). Statement of Kingsley Davis.
15. 3 *Population and Development: Research in Population and Development: Needs and Capacities: Hearings Before the Select Committee on Population,* 95th Cong., 2nd Sess. 488, 525-26 (1978). Second annual report of the National Security Council Ad Hoc Group on Population Policy.
16. D. C. Jayasuriya, Legal Dimensions of Population Dynamics: Perspectives from Asian Countries 143 (Mt. Lavinia, Sri Lanka: Associated Educational Publishers, 1979).
17. These years include all of the work of the 92d Congress through the 95th Congress.
18. Pub. L. No. 95-192, 91 Stat. 1407. By its own terms, the act will expire at the end of 1985. *Id.* at § 10.
19. H. R. Rep. No. 95-344, 95th Cong., 1st Sess. 7, *reprinted in* [1977] U.S. Code Congressional & Administrative News 3670, 3673.
20. Council on Environmental Quality, *Environmental Quality* 270 (ninth annual report; Washington, D.C.: U.S. Gov't. Printing Office, 1978); Lester R. Brown, The Twenty-Ninth Day 135 (New York: Norton, 1978).
21. Council on Environmental Quality, *supra* note 20; Council on Environmental Quality, *Environmental Quality,* 390, 396 (tenth annual report; Washington, D.C.: U.S. Gov't. Printing Office, 1979).
22. Lester R. Brown, *The Worldwide Loss of Cropland* 22-26 (Washington, D.C.: Worldwatch Institute Paper No. 24, 1978); Erik Eckholm, Losing Ground (New York: Norton, 1976).
The Food and Agriculture Act of 1977, Pub. L. No. 95-113, § 1511, 91 Stat. 913, 1022, created a program to combat soil erosion in the Great Plains region. The legislation was a response to serious wind erosion of 6.8 million acres of land, of which approximately 80 percent was cropland, and to the threat of erosion on an additional 17 million acres. The erosion was partly the result of the cultivation of marginal lands during a drought. The influence of population growth is found in a succinct statement in the report on the bill by the House of Representatives: "Prior to being settled and farmed, the Great Plains suffered only slight erosion as natural grasses provided protection from wind and water erosion." H. R. Rep. No. 95-348, 95th Cong., 1st Sess. 37, *reprinted in* [1977] U.S. Code Congressional & Administrative News 1704, 1738.
23. Council on Environmental Quality, *supra* note 20, at 274.
24. Bureau of the Census, U.S. Department of Commerce, Statistical Abstract of the United States: 1980 209 (101st ed.; Washington, D.C.: U.S. Gov't. Printing Office, 1980).
25. Council on Environmental Quality, *supra* note 20, at 270, 272.
26. Pub. L. No. 95-307, 92 Stat. 353.
27. Pub. L. No. 95-514, 92 Stat. 1803.

28. General Accounting Office, Public Rangelands Continue to Deteriorate 4 (Washington, D.C.: U.S. Gov't. Printing Office, 1977).
29. Public Rangelands Improvement Act of 1978, Pub. L. No. 95-514, § 2(3), 92 Stat. 1803; Eckholm, *supra* note 22.
30. Pub. L. No. 94-588, 90 Stat. 2949.
31. Senate Agriculture & Forestry Comm., National Forest Management Act of 1976, S. Rep. No. 94-893, 94th Cong., 2d Sess. 9-10, *reprinted in* [1976] U.S. Code Congressional & Administrative News 6662, 6670.
32. Council on Environmental Quality, *supra* note 20, at 293, 320-21; Council on Environmental Quality & Department of State, 2 *The Global 2000 Report to the President* 123-24 (Washington, D.C.: U.S. Gov't. Printing Office, 1980).
33. Erik Eckholm, *Planting for the Future: Forestry for Human Needs* 5 (Washington, D.C.: Worldwatch Institute Paper No. 26, 1979); Georg Borgstrom, Too Many 1-17 (New York: Macmillan, 1969).
34. Federal Water Pollution Control Act Amendments of 1972, Pub. L. No. 92-500, 86 Stat. 816; Safe Drinking Water Act, Pub. L. No. 93-523, 88 Stat. 1660; Clean Water Act of 1977, Pub. L. No. 95-217, 91 Stat. 1566.
35. Council on Environmental Quality, *Environmental Quality* 394 (eleventh annual report; Washington, D.C.: U.S. Gov't. Printing Office, 1980). The sums cited are in terms of purchasing power in 1979 and will be increased by inflation.
36. *See* Council on Environmental Quality, *Environmental Quality* 76-89 (tenth annual report; Washington, D.C.: U.S. Gov't. Printing Office, 1979); Arnold Reitze, Environmental Law, 2d ed., four-8 (Washington, D.C.: North American International, 1972); *Staff Report to the National Comm'n on Water Quality* IV-25-IV-30 (Washington, D.C.: National Commission on Water Quality, 1976).
37. Bureau of the Census, U.S. Department of Commerce, *Estimates of the Population of the United States to January 1, 1980,* Current Population Reports, Series P-25, No. 878 (1980).
38. Council on Environmental Quality, *supra* note 35, at 100.
39. Soil and Water Resource Conservation Act of 1977, Pub. L. No. 95-192, 91 Stat. 1407; Water Research and Development Act of 1978, Pub. L. No. 95-467, 92 Stat. 1305; Saline Water Conversion Act of 1971, Pub. L. No. 92-60, 85 Stat. 159.
40. Colorado River Basin Salinity Control Act, Pub. L. No. 93-320, 88 Stat. 266.

Human use has increased salt levels in the Colorado River principally through diverting water to agricultural irrigation; water used for irrigation removes salt from soil and returns it to the river. In addition, municipal and industrial consumption has raised the salinity of the water. S. Rep. No. 93-906, 93d Cong., 2d Sess., *reprinted in* [1974] U.S. Code Congressional & Administrative News 3327, 3331.

41. Borgstrom, *supra* note 33, at 153, 159.
42. Ronald Ridker, *Future Water Needs and Supplies, with a Note on Land*

*Use,* in Population, Resources, and the Environment 213, 221-22 (Vol. III of the Research Reports of the U.S. Commission on Population Growth & the American Future, Ronald Ridker, ed.; Washington, D.C.: U.S. Gov't Printing Office, 1972). *See* Council on Environmental Quality & Department of State, *supra* note 32, at 156.

43. Pub. L. No. 95-616, 92 Stat. 3110.
44. Pub. L. No. 93-205, 87 Stat. 884.
45. Act of Dec. 15, 1971, Pub. L. No. 92-195, 85 Stat. 649.
46. Erik Eckholm, *Disappearing Species: The Social Challenge* 6 (Washington, D.C.: Worldwatch Institute Paper No. 22, 1978); Council on Environmental Quality, *supra* note 20, at 328, 334.
47. Eckholm, *supra* note 46, at 18.
48. Council on Environmental Quality, *Environmental Quality* 182-84, 324-27 (fifth annual report; Washington, D.C.: U.S. Gov't. Printing Office, 1974). Quotation from page 325.
49. Pub. L. No. 92-583, 86 Stat. 1280.
50. Pub. L. No. 92-522, 86 Stat. 1027.
51. Pub. L. No. 92-532, 86 Stat. 1052.
52. Pub. L. No. 93-627, 88 Stat. 2126.
53. Pub. L. No. 92-340, 86 Stat. 424.
54. Council on Environmental Quality, *supra* note 36, at 450.
55. Coastal Zone Management Act of 1972, Pub. L. No. 92-583, § 302(c), 86 Stat. 1280. *Accord,* House Merchant Marine & Fisheries Committee, Marine Mammal Protection Act of 1972, H.R. Rep. No. 92-707, 92d Cong., 2d Sess., *reprinted in* [1972] U.S. Code Congressional & Administrative News 4144, 4147.
56. *See* Edward Hudson & Dale Jorgenson, *Energy Prices and the U.S. Economy, 1972-1976,* 18 Natural Resources Journal 877 (1978).
57. Council on Environmental Quality, *Environmental Quality* 298 (eighth annual report; Washington, D.C.: U.S. Gov't Printing Office, 1977).
58. In 1977, the less-developed countries contained three-fourths of the world's population and had a rate of natural increase three times faster than that in the more-developed countries. In the last quarter of the twentieth century, the numerical increment in less-developed regions will be about ten times larger than that in the more-developed regions. Bureau of the Census, U.S. Department of Commerce, World Population 1977 15 (Washington, D.C.: U.S. Gov't. Printing Office, 1978); Council on Environmental Quality & Department of State, *supra* note 32, at 12.
59. Committee on Mineral Resources and the Environment, National Research Council, Mineral Resources and the Environment 26 (Washington, D.C.: National Academy of Sciences, 1975).
60. National Commission on Supplies & Shortages Act of 1974, Pub. L. No. 93-426, 88 Stat. 1167. In section 720(b), Congress explicitly notes an increasing dependence on foreign countries for vital natural resources and an increasing frequency of resource shortages.
61. Pub. L. No. 94-580, 90 Stat. 2795.

62. House Interstate & Foreign Commerce Committee, Solid Waste Disposal Act, H.R. Rep. No. 94-1491, 94th Cong., 2d Sess. 3, *reprinted in* [1976] U.S. Code Congressional & Administrative News 6238, 6241.

63. Donald Brobst & Walden Pratt, *Introduction*, in United States Mineral Resources 1, 7 (Donald A. Brobst & Walden Pratt, eds.; Washington, D.C.: U.S. Gov't. Printing Office, 1973).

64. *E.g.*, Emergency Daylight Saving Time Energy Conservation Act of 1973, Pub. L. No. 93-182, 87 Stat. 707; Energy Supply and Environmental Coordination Act of 1974, Pub. L. No. 93-319, 88 Stat. 246; Geothermal Energy Research, Development, and Demonstration Act of 1974, Pub. L. No. 93-410, 88 Stat. 1079; Solar Energy Research, Development, and Demonstration Act of 1974, Pub. L. No. 93-473, 88 Stat. 1431; Electric and Hybrid Vehicle Research, Development, and Demonstration Act of 1976, Pub. L. No. 94-413, 90 Stat. 1260; Surface Mining Control and Reclamation Act of 1977, Pub. L. No. 95-87, 91 Stat. 445; Energy Tax Act of 1978, Pub. L. No. 95-618, 92 Stat. 3174; National Energy Conservation Policy Act, Pub. L. No. 95-619, 92 Stat. 3206; National Gas Policy Act of 1978, Pub. L. No. 95-621, 92 Stat. 3350.

65. House Interstate & Foreign Commerce Committee, Energy Policy and Conservation Act, H.R. Rep. No. 94-340, 94th Cong., 1st Sess. 1, *reprinted in* [1975] U.S. Code Congressional & Administrative News 1762, 1763.

66. Brobst & Pratt, *supra* note 63, at 8.

67. Patrick Nolan, *Size and Administrative Intensity in Nations*, 44 American Sociological Review 110 (1979).

68. Flood Disaster Protection Act of 1973, Pub. L. No. 93-234, 87 Stat. 975; Disaster Relief Act of 1974, Pub. L. No. 93-288, 88 Stat. 143; Community Emergency Drought Relief Act of 1977, Pub. L. No. 95-31, 91 Stat. 169; Food and Agriculture Act of 1977, Pub. L. No. 95-113, § 1103, 91 Stat. 953.

69. National Weather Modification Policy Act of 1976, Pub. L. No. 94-490, 90 Stat. 2359.

70. Pub. L. No. 95-367, 92 Stat. 601.

71. *Id.* at § 2(1).

72. Pub. L. No. 95-124, 91 Stat. 1098.

73. *Id.* at § 2(2).

74. Commission on Population Growth & the American Future, Population and the American Future 41 (Washington, D.C.: U.S. Gov't. Printing Office, 1972); Thomas Espenshade, *Zero Population Growth and the Economies of Developed Nations*, 4 Population & Development Review 645 (1978).

75. *Some Economic Consequences of a Declining Population*, 4 Population & Development Review 517, 522 (1978).

76. Dianne Wolman, *Findings of the Commission's National Public Opinion Survey*, in Aspects of Population Growth Policy 469, 480 (Vol. VI of the Research Reports of the U.S. Commission on Population Growth and the American Future, Charles F. Westoff & Robert Parke, Jr., eds.; Washington, D.C.: U.S. Gov't. Printing Office, 1972).

The question asked was "Do you agree or disagree with those who claim that population growth helps keep our economy prosperous?" Among all respondents, 52 percent disagreed, 36 percent agreed, and 12 percent registered no opinion. The proportion disagreeing was substantially higher for whites than for blacks (53 and 38 percent, respectively) and increased with educational level (from 45 percent among those who had not graduated from high school to 66 percent among those who had graduated from college).

77. Act of October 27, 1972, Pub. L. No. 92-597, 86 Stat. 1319; Comprehensive Employment and Training Act of 1973, Pub. L. No. 93-203, 87 Stat. 839; Emergency Jobs and Unemployment Assistance Act of 1974, Pub. L. No. 93-567, 88 Stat. 1845; Comprehensive Employment and Training Act Amendments of 1978, Pub. L. No. 95-524, 92 Stat. 1909; Economic Opportunity Amendments of 1978, Pub. L. No. 95-568, 92 Stat. 2425; Youth Employment and Demonstration Projects Act of 1977, Pub. L. No. 95-93, 91 Stat. 627.

78. Pub. L. No. 95-523, 92 Stat. 1887.
79. *Id.* at § 205(a) (1).
80. Bureau of the Census, *supra* note 24, at 30.
81. *Id.* at 407.
82. Pub. L. No. 95-390, 92 Stat. 755.
83. House Post Office & Civil Service Committee, Federal Employees Flexible and Compressed Work Schedules Act of 1978, H.R. Rep. No. 95-912, 95th Cong., 2d Sess. 11, *reprinted in* [1978] U.S. Code Congressional & Administrative News 3300, 3309.
84. I.R.C. §§ 151(e), 152(a), (1979) (amended by Pub. L. No. 95-600, § 102(a), 92 Stat. 2771).
85. Senate Finance Committee, Revenue Act of 1978, S. Rep. No. 95-1263, 95th Cong., 2d Sess. 46, *reprinted in* [1978] U.S. Code Congressional & Administrative News 6761, 6809.
86. *See generally* Hudson & Jorgenson, *supra* note 56.
87. Brown, *supra* note 20, at 161-91.
88. State & Local Fiscal Assistance Act of 1972, Pub. L. No. 92-512, 86 Stat. 919.
89. Senate Finance Committee, State and Local Fiscal Assistance Act of 1972, S. Rep. No. 92-1050, 92d Cong., 2d Sess., *reprinted in* [1972] U.S. Code Congressional & Administrative News 3874, 3882.
90. Pub. L. No. 95-24, 91 Stat. 56.
91. *Id.* at § 202(b).
92. Pub. L. No. 95-557, 92 Stat. 2122.
93. Pub. L. No. 95-625, 92 Stat. 3538.
94. Pub. L. No. 94-580, 90 Stat. 2795.
95. House Interstate & Foreign Commerce Committee, Solid Waste Disposal Act, H.R. Rep. No. 94-1491, 94th Cong., 2d Sess. 3, *reprinted in* [1976] U.S. Code Congressional & Administrative News 6238, 6240.

The Supreme Court has held that, because the Constitution assigns the power to regulate interstate commerce to Congress, a state cannot prohibit the disposal of waste on privately owned land within its jurisdiction simply because the waste has been brought from another state. City of Philadelphia v New Jersey, 437 U.S. 518 (1978).

96. Anthony Downs, *Housing Markets and Big-City Population Losses,* in House Select Committee on Population, 3 Consequences of Changing U.S. Population: Population Movement and Planning, 95th Cong., 2d Sess. 218, 222 (1978); James D. Williams & Andrew Sofranko, *Motivations for the Inmigration Component of Population Turnaround in Nonmetropolitan Areas,* 16 Demography 239 (1979).

97. Jay Forrester, *Counterintuitive Behavior of Social Systems,* 73 Technology Review 1, 6 (1971).

98. Pub. L. No. 93-449, 88 Stat. 1364.

99. Pub. L. No. 94-50, 89 Stat. 249.

100. Hudson & Jorgenson, *supra* note 56.

101. Task Force on Homeownership, *Hearings before the Subcommittee on Housing & Community Development of the House Committee on Banking, Finance & Urban Affairs,* 95th Cong., 2d Sess. 900 (1978). Statement of Gary Baxter.

102. *Id.* at 460 (statement of Dale Stuard) and 617 (statement of Michael Matrix).

103. *Id.* at 900 (statement of Gary Baxter).

104. *Id.* at 481 (statement of Fred Case).

As the result of the natural increase of the population following World War II, approximately 875,000 new households were formed annually between 1970 and 1978, creating a substantial demand for new housing and more energy. Bureau of the Census, U.S. Department of Commerce, *Projections of the Number of Households and Families: 1979 to 1995,* Current Population Reports, Series P-25, No. 805, at 5 (1979).

105. Pub. L. No. 95-113, 91 Stat. 981.

106. *See* House Agricultural Committee, Food and Agriculture Act of 1977, H.R. Rep. No. 95-348, 95th Cong., 1st Sess. 103, *reprinted in* [1977] U.S. Code Congressional & Administrative News 1704, 1804.

107. Pub. L. No. 95-113, 91 Stat. 958.

108. *Id.* at § 5(a), 91 Stat. 962.

109. National School Lunch & Child Nutrition Act Amendments of 1973, Pub. L. No. 93-150, 87 Stat. 560; National School Lunch Act & Child Nutrition Amendments of 1977, Pub. L. No. 95-166, 91 Stat. 1325; Child Nutrition Amendments of 1978, Pub. L. No. 95-627, 92 Stat. 3603. *Accord,* Act of November 5, 1971, Pub. L. No. 92-153, 85 Stat. 419.

110. Child Nutrition Amendments of 1978, Pub. L. No. 95-627, § 3, 92 Stat. 3611.

111. Brown, *supra* note 20, at 128-91; Brown, *supra* note 22; Lester R. Brown, By Bread Alone (New York: Praeger, 1974); Eckholm, *supra* note 22.

112. James Smith & Finis Welch, *No Time to Be Young: The Economic Prospects for Large Cohorts in the United States,* 7 Population and Develop-

ment Review 71 (1981); Richard Freeman, *The Effect of the Youth Population on the Wages of Young Workers,* in House Select Committee on Population, 2 Consequences of Changing U.S. Population: Baby Boom and Bust, 95th Cong., 2d Sess. 767, 775 (1978); Lindert, *supra* note 6, at 216-59.

113. Bureau of the Census, U.S. Department of Commerce, *Characteristics of the Population Below the Poverty Level: 1978,* Current Population Reports, Series P-60, No. 124, at 51, 63 (1980).

114. Lindert, *supra* note 6, at 214-15; Dennis De Tray, Child Schooling and Family Size: An Economic Analysis 36 (Santa Monica, Calif.: Rand Corporation, 1978); *see* Judith Blake, *The Only Child in America: Prejudice versus Performance,* 7 Population and Development Review 43, 50-51 (1981).

115. Noise Control Act of 1972, Pub. L. No. 92-574, 86 Stat. 1234; Quiet Communities Act of 1978, Pub. L. No. 95-609, 92 Stat. 3079.

116. Senate Public Works Committee, Noise Control Act of 1972, S. Rep. No. 92-1160, 92d Cong., 2d Sess., *reprinted in* [1972] U.S. Code Congressional & Administrative News 4655, 4656; Council on Environmental Quality, *supra* note 36, at 537-38.

117. Council on Environmental Quality, *supra* note 36, at 544.

118. Pub. L. No. 92-516, 86 Stat. 973.

119. Senate Agriculture & Forestry Committee, Federal Environmental Pesticide Control Act of 1972, S. Rep. No. 92-838, 92d Cong., 2d Sess., *reprinted in* [1972] U.S. Code Congressional & Administrative News 3993, 3995-98.

120. Pub. L. No. 92-218, 85 Stat. 778.

121. Erik Eckholm, The Picture of Health 33 (New York: Norton, 1977).

122. Child Abuse Prevention & Treatment Act, Pub. L. No. 93-247, 88 Stat. 4; Juvenile Justice & Delinquency Prevention Act of 1974, Pub. L. No. 93-415, tit. III, 88 Stat. 1129.

123. Walter Gove, Michael Hughes, & Omer Galle, *Overcrowding in the Home: An Empirical Investigation of Its Possible Pathological Consequences,* 44 American Sociological Review 59 (1979).

124. Forrester, *supra* note 97; *see* Albert Chevan, *Family Growth, Household Density, and Moving,* 8 Demography 451 (1971).

125. William R. Catton, Jr., Overshoot (Urbana: University of Illinois Press, 1980).

# 3 POPULATION GROWTH AND THE RIGHT OF PRIVACY

In the preceding chapter we examined the wide variety of problems that population increase has helped create in the United States. This chapter discusses one more deleterious effect of population increase — this one, of a constitutional nature. The chapter argues that population growth has reduced the privacy of American citizens and has thereby circumvented, and in effect decreased, the protections afforded by the constitutional right of privacy.

## CONSTITUTIONAL RIGHT OF PRIVACY

A right of privacy is not expressly mentioned in the Constitution. However, the Supreme Court has held that a right of privacy protecting decisions about childbearing is implicit in the due process clauses of the Fifth and Fourteenth Amendments, which forbid federal and state governments from engaging in actions depriving any person of "liberty without due process of law."[1] The liberty guarantee shields the individual from unnecessary governmental interference in the decision whether to have a child.[2] "If the right of privacy means anything," the Court has stated, "it is the right of the individual, married or single, to be free of unwarranted governmental intrusion into matters so fundamentally affecting a person as the decision whether to bear or beget a child."[3] The right of privacy has been used to invalidate legislation imposing a total ban on abortions or requiring a husband's consent to his wife's having an abortion.[4]

Unfortunately, the Court does not appear to appreciate at least one important ramification of the right of privacy. On two recent occasions it has held that government is not constitutionally required to pay the expenses of abortions for indigent women, even when it pays the expenses of childbirth.[5] Government is thus able to provide an inducement to carry a pregnancy to term even for women who might otherwise not do so, and thus government effectively encourages unnecessary population growth.[6] Indeed, the Court explicitly recognized that encouragement of population growth was a governmental interest that justified not paying for medically unnecessary abortions.[7] The Court's viewpoint was especially noteworthy because the government had never contended that population growth was a goal of the policy being challenged;[8] the Court therefore had no reason to make a statement on the matter except to express the view of its majority that population increase is beneficial. Ironically, population growth has forced government to impose, or at least to permit, coercive influences on fertility and to restrict the ability of individuals to decide freely on the number of children they will have. In holding that the right of privacy is not implicated when government encourages childbearing, the Court did not consider or understand the limitations that population growth imposes on decisions about family size.

## CASES INVOLVING POPULATION GROWTH AND THE RIGHT OF PRIVACY

The manner in which population pressures frustrate the protections afforded by the right of privacy and limit childbearing freedom is well illustrated by a Maryland court case. The owner of a parcel of land zoned for multiple-family/medium-density housing sought a special exception from the county in order to construct apartment buildings containing more bedrooms than were permitted under the zoning ordinance applicable to the area.[9] The owner proposed to build apartments with a total of 442 bedrooms, but the zoning ordinance allowed only 367. The county denied the application on the ground that school facilities could not handle the additional students that would accompany the larger number of bedrooms. The owner, filing suit, claimed that the ordinance was an unreasonable restriction on private property unrelated to the general welfare, and created an unconstitutional distinction between large and small families. In response to the first argument, the court held that zoning to regulate population density was a valid exercise of the police power possessed by states and their subdivisions to promote the general welfare and that, given the rapid growth of population occurring in the region, the ordinance was a reasonable means to control density. In response to the argument that large families would be limited in their ability to locate suitable housing while small families would not, the court held that the owner had failed to prove that the distinction between large and small families was unreasonable.

While it might be argued that the zoning ordinance increased privacy by reducing density, the argument overlooks the impact of limited bedroom space on the ability to decide freely on the number of children one wishes to have. Individuals contemplating additional children will be deterred from having them if they cannot obtain housing with a sufficient number of bedrooms.[10] Therefore, the zoning ordinance was in effect a governmental measure influencing the number of children a couple could have. That measure, in turn, stemmed from the fact that the population levels permitted under the ordinance were evidently the maximum that the school system could handle. Because population numbers were threatening to exceed the ability of the social system to provide educational facilities, government adopted a measure that, intentionally or unintentionally, restricted the number of children that parents could decide to have. The right of privacy, however, was intended to minimize governmental interference in such decisions.

We can find other illustrations of the manner in which population growth has reduced privacy, restricted individuals in their ability to have children, and thus frustrated the protections afforded by the right of privacy. A number of court cases have resulted from population increases that have created the need for housing of greater density. In these cases the courts have held that there is no right to low-density housing—nor, consequently, to greater privacy—when the community is experiencing pressures from population growth. As a result, government has been required to permit or promote housing of high density and limited space—which, as we have seen, acts to curb fertility.[11] For example, in a Pennsylvania case a township in the path of population expansion from two directions amended its zoning ordinance to require a minimum of four acres of land for each lot on which there was to be residential construction.[12] The owner of a parcel of land proposed to build single-family homes on lots of one acre each, a plan that would have been acceptable under the zoning applicable to the land prior to the amendment. When denied a building permit for construction on one-acre lots, the owner filed suit challenging the constitutionality of the four-acre minimum. The Supreme Court of Pennsylvania recognized the desirability of large lots in terms of reducing or eliminating the problems of congestion, pollution, and shortages of natural resources and governmental services but pointed out that the police power under which governments zone must be utilized to achieve public purposes rather than private preferences. The police power, the court found, must promote the welfare of the public at large and not the purely selfish interests of the individual. The court concluded that the four-acre lot requirement was not necessary to the welfare of the public but merely manifested an impermissible private desire to exclude population increments:

> Zoning is a tool in the hands of governmental bodies which enables them to more effectively meet the demands of evolving and growing communities. It must not and cannot be used by those officials as an instrument by which they may shirk their responsibilities. Zoning is a means by which a governmental body can plan for the future—it may not be used as a means to deny the future....
>
> There is no doubt that many of the residents of this area are highly desirous of keeping it the way it is, preferring, quite naturally, to look out upon land in its natural state rather than on other homes. These desires, however, do not rise to the level of public welfare. This is purely a matter of private desire which zoning regulations may not be employed to effectuate.[13]

Thus, when it is not fully developed,[14] a community must face the problem of population growth and meet it as best it can, even when the population increments come from other areas.[15] However, a locality is not able to maintain even the low density of single-family homes on one-acre lots if higher density is necessary to provide housing. Accordingly, a community that is developing must accept its fair share of apartments if there are people in the region who need such housing.[16]

Population density and space limitations in housing are not the only factors that act to curtail childbearing. Experimental evidence from lower animal species indicates that noise can have the same effect.[17] As population numbers rise, the level of noise in an industrialized, urbanized society will also increase.[18] Let us look at two recent cases that arose from noise-generating facilities constructed by government as the result of population pressures. Both cases involved claims by landowners that, because of the noise, their property had in effect been appropriated by government and that they were therefore entitled to financial compensation. In neither case were damages awarded, but even if they had been, there would have been no diminution in noise levels. The cases serve to illustrate situations where citizens have been unable to obtain relief for injury caused by intrusion into the privacy of the home of noise that stemmed from government-constructed facilities—noise that ultimately was generated by population growth and that could have curtailed childbearing.

In the first case the plaintiff owners resided in a house near which the defendant state had built an interstate highway and access road.[19] Though none of their land was taken in eminent domain proceedings, the plaintiffs sought to compel the state to provide compensation for damages to their house and for loss of solitude. Specifically, they alleged that their physical and mental health had been impaired because of a high and continuing level of noise from traffic and that vibrations from the use of construction equipment had caused severe structural damage to their house. In ruling for the state and holding that the plaintiffs did not have a cause of action, the court relied on the general rule applied to a situation where there has been damage to property, no part of which has been subjected to physical intrusion and use:

Acts done in the proper exercise of governmental powers, and not directly encroaching upon private property, though their consequences may impair its use, are universally held not to be [a] taking within the meaning of the constitutional provision [under which private property may be taken only for a public purpose and with full compensation to the owner]. If the property owner's annoyance is of the same type to which everyone living in the vicinity is subjected in varying degrees there is, at most, a sharing in the common burden of incidental damages.[20]

The second case applied the same principle in a different setting. The case arose when a city board of education exercised its eminent domain powers to acquire part of the defendants' land to build a junior high school.[21] The board appealed a jury award of four thousand dollars for damages to the portion of the land that had not been taken and that contained the defendants' home. The jury had presumably granted the compensation at least in part because of the noise emanating from the school, but the state supreme court eliminated the award on the ground that there had been no physical intrusion by government onto the land and that the defendants had not suffered any damage differing from that sustained by the public generally.

The preceding cases occurred in the context of zoning and eminent domain and involved a reduction in privacy stemming from population pressures. We have seen that diminished privacy from population increases can act to restrict fertility, but in ways that do not infringe the constitutional right of privacy that was designed to protect childbearing decisions.

Let us now turn to a different context and examine tort cases in which landowners whose privacy was reduced by population growth made unsuccessful allegations of nuisance.

## TORT LAW AND THE RIGHT OF PRIVACY

Tort law recognizes two types of nuisance—namely, public and private; the difference between them lies in the pervasiveness of the effect of the activity in question. A public nuisance is one affecting a considerable portion of a community; a private nuisance is one affecting a small number of individuals in a way that differs from the effect on the community at large. It appears to be generally held that an activity conducted in compliance with existing zoning regulations or pursuant to authorizing legislation is not a public nuisance that the courts can enjoin. Compliance with regulations is a persuasive factor in judicial decisions against the prohibition of an activity as a private nuisance.[22] Accordingly, the Supreme Court of Colorado held that the noise and air pollution created by a limestone mining operation carried on in full compliance with state statutes and local zoning ordinances did not constitute a public nuisance.[23] Also, the Supreme Court of Pennsylvania ruled that construction of a state-authorized dam was not a public nuisance even if allegations were true that the effects of construction would include elimination of recreational facilities, increased traffic congestion, and health hazards.[24]

In both of the preceding cases population pressures generated an increased demand for resources (mining products in one case and water in the other), which led to government approval of mining and of water control projects. At the same time, population pressures also forced people to live in areas near the objectionable projects. In turn, the increased noise and congestion stemming from the government-sanctioned projects intruded on the privacy of individuals and potentially affected childbearing decisions.

## ENERGY SHORTAGES AND THE RIGHT OF PRIVACY

Finally, let us consider the ramifications of energy shortages, since they involve the federal government rather than, as in the material presented above, local governments. One result of energy shortages will be to force individuals to live in communities of relatively high population density, because such communities consume substantially less energy for cooling and heating dwellings and for transportation than do communities of low density.[25] Federal law is already moving the nation in the direction of high-density communities. The Department of Housing and Urban Development, for example, is required by statute to encourage plans and programs that conserve natural resources in providing grants for urban planning to state and local governments.[26] Regulations issued by the department provide for the development of land-use plans that control the distribution of people in order to minimize energy consumption.[27]

Since the department was one of the sponsors of the study finding that high-density housing reduced energy consumption, it will evidently promote plans for such housing. In doing so, however, the department is also reducing privacy and thereby, it seems, discouraging people from bearing children, even though the constitutional right of privacy implies that decisions about childbearing should be made with a maximum of freedom from governmental controls.

## NOTES

1. The due process clause of the Fifth Amendment applies to the federal government, while that of the Fourteenth Amendment applies to states and their subdivisions.
2. Carey v Population Serv. Int'l, 431 U.S. 678 (1977).
3. *Id.* at 685.
4. Roe v Wade, 410 U.S. 113 (1973); Planned Parenthood of Central Missouri v Danforth, 428 U.S. 52 (1976).
5. Maher v Roe, 432 U.S. 464 (1977); Harris v McRae, 100 S.Ct. 2671 (1980).
6. The number of births that will occur as the result of limitations on public funds for abortions for indigents is not known. *Compare* Richard Lincoln, Brigitte Döring-Bradley, Barbara Lindheim, & Maureen Cotterill, *The Court, the Congress and the President: Turning Back the Clock on the Pregnant Poor,* 9 Family Planning Perspectives 207, 212, 213 (1977) *with* James Trussell, Jane Menken, Barbara Lindheim, & Barbara Vaughan, *The Impact of Restricting Medicaid Financing for Abortion,* 12 Family Planning Perspectives 120 (1980).
7. "[A] State may have legitimate demographic concerns about its rate of population growth. Such concerns are basic to the future of the State and in some circumstances could constitute a substantial reason for departure from a position of neutrality between abortion and childbirth." 432 U.S. at 478 n.11.
8. 432 U.S. at 489n. (Brennan, Marshall, & Blackmun, JJ, dissenting).
9. Malmar Associates v Bd. of County Comm'rs, 260 Md. 292, 272 A.2d 6 (1971).
10. Space limitations and crowding have a major effect in curtailing family size. Marcus Felson & M. Solaun, *The Fertility-Inhibiting Effect of Crowded Apartment Living in a Tight Housing Market,* 80 American Journal of Sociology 1410 (1975); James P. Curry & Gayle Scriven, *The Relationship between Apartment Living and Fertility for Blacks, Mexican-Americans, and Other Americans in Racine, Wisconsin,* 15 Demography 477 (1978); Edward T. Hall, The Hidden Dimension 15–39 (Garden City, N.Y.: Doubleday, 1969); Joseph R. Lombardi & John A. Vanderbergh, *Pheromonally Induced Sexual Maturation in Females: Regulation by the Social Environment of the Male,* 196 Science 545 (1977).

11. *Id.*
12. Nat'l Land & Inv. Co. v Kohn, 419 Pa. 504, 215 A.2d 597 (1965).
13. *Id.* at 610, 611.
14. Pascack Ass'n, Ltd. v Mayor & Council of Washington, 74 N.J. 470, 379 A.2d 6 (1977); Surrick v Zoning Hearing Bd., 476 Pa. 182, 382 A.2d 105 (1977).
15. Appeal of Kit-Mar Builders, Inc., 439 Pa. 466, 268 A.2d 765, 768 (1970); So. Burlington County N.A.A.C.P. v Twp. of Mt. Laurel, 67 N.J. 151, 336 A.2d 713 (1975), *appeal dismissed for want of jurisdiction,* 423 U.S. 808 (1975); Oakwood at Madison, Inc. v Twp. of Madison, 117 N.J. 11, 283 A.2d 353 (Super. Ct. 1971); Berenson v Town of New Castle, 38 N.Y.2d 102, 378 N.Y.S.2d 672 (1975); Bd. of County Supervisors v Carper, 200 Va. 653, 107 S.E.2d 390 (1959).
16. Twp. of Williston v Chesterdale Farms, Inc., 341 A.2d 466 (Pa. 1975); Surrick v Zoning Hearing Bd., *supra* note 14.
17. A. Arvay, *Effect of Noise During Pregnancy Upon Fetal Viability and Development,* in Physiological Effects of Noise 91 (Bruce L. Welch & Annemarrie Welch, eds.; New York: Plenum, 1970); William Geber, *Cardiovascular and Teratogenic Effects of Chronic Intermittent Noise Stress,* in *id.* at 85; I. Tamari, *Audiogenic Stimulation and Reproduction Function,* in *id.* at 117.
18. Council on Environmental Quality, Environmental Quality 544 (tenth annual report; Washington, D.C.: U.S. Gov't. Printing Office, 1979).
19. Northcutt v State Road Dep't, 209 So.2d 710 (Fla. Dist. Ct. App. 1968), *cert. discharged,* 219 So.2d 687 (Fla. 1969).
20. *Id.* at 713. This quotation was taken from a treatise, the current citation for which is 4A Nichols' The Law of Eminent Domain § 14.1[1] (3rd ed. rev.; New York: Mathew Bender, 1979).
21. Bd. of Educ. v Croft, 13 Utah2d 310, 373 P.2d 697 (1962). *Accord,* Mayfield v Bd. of Educ., 118 Kan. 138, 233 P. 1024 (1925).
22. Desruisseau v Isley, 27 Ariz. App. 257, 553 P.2d 1242, 1246 (Ct. App. 1976); Clabaugh v Harris, 27 Ohio Misc. 153, 273 N.E.2d 923 (Ct. C.P. 1971).
23. Green v Castle Concrete Co., 509 P.2d 588 (Colo. 1973).
24. Borough of Collegeville v Philadelphia Suburban Water Co., 377 Pa. 636, 105 A.2d 722 (1954).
25. Real Estate Research Corporation, The Costs of Sprawl 5, 13 (Washington, D.C.: U.S. Gov't. Printing Office, 1974); Council on Environmental Quality, *Environmental Quality* 15-19 (fifth annual report; Washington, D.C.: U.S. Gov't. Printing Office, 1974).
26. 40 U.S.C. § 461(n) (1976).
27. 24 C.F.R. § 600.72(a) (1980).

# II SOME FACTORS AFFECTING CHILDBEARING

# 4 CONSTITUTIONAL LAW AND "THE TRAGEDY OF THE COMMONS"

Part II is concerned with the constitutional dimension of factors that appear to have an impact on fertility decisions and family size. The impact of these factors, which is largely unintentional, is not generally recognized—therefore, the factors and their constitutional dimensions are all the more important. In this chapter we focus on a factor that forms the basis of a line of scientific research that is just commencing but holds the promise of affecting public policy on a wide variety of issues, including population. The factor is a phenomenon associated with goods and services that are owned by the public and thus shared in common. Biologist Garrett Hardin has termed the phenomenon "the tragedy of the commons" and has illustrated it as follows:

> Picture a pasture open to all. It is to be expected that each herdsman will try to keep as many cattle as possible on the commons.... As a rational being, each herdsman seeks to minimize his gain [and thus] the rational herdsman concludes that the only sensible course for him to pursue is to add another animal to his herd. And another.... But this is the conclusion reached by each and every rational herdsman sharing a commons. Therein is the tragedy. Each man is locked into a system that compels him to increase

his herd without limit—in a world that is limited. Ruin is the destination toward which all men rush, each pursuing his own best interest in a society that believes in the freedom of the commons.[1]

"The tragedy of the commons" is that publicly owned goods and publicly operated services tend to be overexploited and, possibly, irreparably damaged as individuals maximize the use of resources without regard to long-term consequences. Overexploitation occurs because individuals do not own public goods and services, and thus their use has no immediate and visible cost. Two possible means exist to prevent overexploitation: The commons can remain under public ownership, but regulations can be imposed that restrict access and use to sustainable levels; or the commons can be eliminated and public goods and services transferred to private ownership. The former approach, which involves governmental controls, is the dominant one in use today. Let us therefore consider the potential consequences of the latter.

## PRIVATE OWNERSHIP AND THE PROTECTION OF RESOURCES

Unfortunately, there has been only limited scientific research on the ability of private ownership to prevent misuse of resources. One study on the yield of lobster fishing areas in Maine differentiated the areas by the degree of private ownership.[2] Areas with a relatively high degree of private ownership yielded larger, more numerous lobsters per fisherman and higher per capita incomes than areas where private ownership was minimal or nonexistent. Another study involved a laboratory experiment in which use of a self-replenishing resource was subjected to varying conditions in order to determine the effect of (1) individual versus common ownership of resources and (2) visibility of resource levels.[3] The optimum strategy for extracting the resource while maximizing its replenishment was most closely approximated when there were both individual ownership and visible resource levels. Significantly, misuse or destruction of a resource appeared not to be avoidable simply with knowledge of the optimum strategy or with information about the manner in which individual conduct would lead to misuse or destruction.[4]

Research thus appears to support the proposition that individual ownership is an essential ingredient in the preservation of a renewable resource. Moreover, it has been found that protection of a resource increases as the members of the group using it communicate with one another;[5] communication among group members, however, becomes more difficult as group size increases. It has also been found that the degree to which individuals cooperate and act responsibly to promote group welfare declines as the size of the group rises.[6] Accordingly, the importance of individual ownership of resources in relation to resource protection appears to increase with population size.

## Private Responsibility and Population Growth

If private ownership and responsibility are more important to conservation as population size mounts, they also seem capable of curtailing population growth. Decisions regarding family size are significantly affected by the personal costs—financial, social, and psychological—that children entail.[7] Parents in our society are able to place a substantial portion of these costs on the public. Thus, parents reduce the burden they would otherwise experience from children, and they may therefore decide to have more children than they would have if they carried the full burden. For instance, publicly funded education removes a major financial burden that, if placed on parents, would undoubtedly depress family size; in 1978-79, the average expenditure per student was $1,900 in public primary and secondary schools.[8] Similarly, an income tax credit for the costs of child care provides a public subsidy that helps both parents to work if they want to do so.[9] The impact of children on family finances and on the ability of both parents to work are factors that limit family size,[10] but public means have been used to attenuate their influence.

Research into the consequences of placing the costs of children on their parents is rare; the relevant work that has been done is not explicitly focused on this issue. While such research will undoubtedly become more frequent in the future, we cannot identify at this point the full range of implications it will have for population policy. However, recent sociological research suggests some implications that can be pursued.

## CONSTITUTIONAL PROTECTION AGAINST THE BURDENS OF CHILDREN

Children and their welfare have increasingly come under the protection of national constitutions. A study of the period from 1870 to 1970 found that the proportion of national constitutions containing express provisions regarding children rose substantially; nation-states increasingly came to recognize childhood as a distinct status and to specify the responsibility of the nation-state for children and their welfare, particularly their education.[11] Two ideological factors were advanced by the authors of the study to explain the trend. First, as societies become technically more advanced, the individual is increasingly seen as a rational being who is the most desirable source of social, political, and economic action; groups such as the family tend to lose their importance in societal ideology. Second, the nation-state is increasingly viewed by its citizens as necessary to the social coordination of individuals and the protection of their welfare. In the words of the authors of the study:

> The dominance of the ideology of differentiated and state-managed childhood reflects the rise of both individualism and the rationalized nation-state. The individual's status in society increasingly takes the form of membership (citizenship) in the nation and state: the individual becomes as much an agent of the collectivity as of personal or subgroup interests. In this vein, modern childhood comes under the authority of the state as part of the state's command over the socialization of its constitutive members—its authority to prepare its citizens for their roles in aiding national development, achieving progress, and obtaining success in the world system [of nations].[12]

The United States stands almost alone among nations in having no provision in its Constitution expressly dealing with children.[13] Nonetheless, given the role of the American judiciary in reviewing statutes and regulations under the Constitution, the welfare of children may have been given increased constitutional protection through judicial decision. If this argument is valid, constitutional adjudication can be said to have effectively promoted childbearing and population growth to the extent that the Constitution has been held (1) to approve governmental action alleviating the burdens that children place on parents or (2) prohibit governmental action that imposes burdens on parents. If either or both of these situations have increased in frequency, judicial interpretation of the Constitution has fostered a milieu—that is, a commons—in which parents can more easily act as free riders on group resources. Individuals need have less concern with the personal consequences of having children as the probability rises that those consequences will not occur. In other words, whether individuals become free riders on group resources is determined by the nature of the milieu in which they find themselves. Parents can more easily decide to have children insofar as the milieu reduces the need for them to consider the possible negative consequences of their decision.

How does the Constitution as construed by the Supreme Court view the burdens of the childrearing process and governmental responsibility for them?[14] At the most general level, the Court has stated that a constitutional wall surrounds the parent-child relationship and that childrearing is the responsibility of the parents unless an overriding public interest intervenes. Thus, the Court in 1978 emphasized:

> We have recognized on numerous occasions that the relationship between parent and child is constitutionally protected. It is cardinal with us that the custody, care and nurture of the child reside first in the parents, whose primary function and freedom include preparation for obligations the state can neither supply nor hinder.[15]

Two issues frequently faced by the Court—illegitimacy and educational costs—permit us to examine how the Court's philosophy works in concrete situations. One would anticipate that, because of a reluctance to permit intrusions into the parent-child relationship, any move by government to place burdens on persons who have illegitimate children will be viewed with disfavor. Moreover, given the primary responsibility of parents for their children, one would expect that the Court would not view with alarm the imposition on parents of the financial costs of educating their children.

## Illegitimacy

Illegitimate births constitute a substantial and increasing share of the total number of births in the United States. The proportion of all births that were illegitimate rose from 4.0 percent in 1950 to 10.7

percent in 1970, and to 16.3 percent in 1978.[16] Illegitimacy thus quadrupled its share of all births between 1950 and 1978. The increase continued steadily, even in the years following the 1973 decision of the Supreme Court that invalidated statutes that prohibited abortion during the first two trimesters of pregnancy.[17] Since illegitimacy continued to increase in the years during which the availability of abortion and the proportion of women wanting abortions who obtained them also increased,[18] the rising incidence of illegitimacy may be attributable in part to insufficient personal penalties for unmarried parenthood.[19]

The pervasiveness and the nature of such penalties is affected by the Constitution and the protections it affords parent-child relationships. Government action that distinguishes between legitimate and illegitimate children encounters the equal protection clause and its restrictions on classifications.[20] Moreover, constitutional protections given to parent-child relationships have been extended to all relationships that individuals choose to establish in a family context, and "the decision whether or not to beget or bear a child is at the very heart of this cluster of constitutionally protected choices."[21] Government action affecting procreation, both illegitimate and legitimate, may violate the right of privacy that stems from the guarantee of liberty contained in the due process clauses of the Constitution and includes fertility decisions.[22] The Supreme Court has formally developed two tests under the due process and equal protection guarantees for evaluating the validity of government statutes, regulations, and practices that affect fertility. The weaker test requires only that what government has done possess a reasonable basis in order to be constitutional, while the stricter test requires that government action be founded on a compelling interest and be no broader than necessary to achieve that interest.[23] The former, or "reasonable basis," test is applied unless government has seriously infringed the right of privacy[24] or has established a "suspect" class—that is, a class "saddled with such disabilities, or subjected to such a history of purposeful unequal treatment, or relegated to such a position of political powerlessness as to command extraordinary protection from the majoritarian political process."[25]

Illegitimate children have not been deemed a suspect class that invokes the stricter test. The Court has employed a intermediate test between the reasonable basis standard and the compelling interest standard at least once, because illegitimacy "classifications approach sensitive and fundamental personal rights"[26] — by which the Court presumably means the right of privacy, since the right protects the individual, regardless of marital status, in making decisions whether to have children.[27] However, on other occasions the Court has indicated that the test is simply one of reasonableness.[28] The standard to be used with regard to government action in the area of illegitimacy is thus not completely clear, but it is certainly not the most restrictive that could be imposed. Nevertheless, apart from the exact nature of the test used, a review of court opinions shows a definite pattern of constitutional limitations placed on governmental action affecting illegitimacy.

Two types of relevant cases exist. In the first, state statutes have placed burdens on illegitimate children or on their parents for the recovery of compensation upon the death of the other. The Court has uniformly invalidated such statutes under the equal protection clause. For example, the Court has struck down a statute permitting legitimate, but not illegitimate, children to recover damages for the wrongful death of their parents on the ground that "[l]egitimacy or illegitimacy of birth has no relation to the nature of the wrong."[29] The Court has invalidated a statute prohibiting the unmarried parents of an illegitimate child from recovering damages for the death of the child, because such a statute "creates an open season on illegitimates"[30] without inhibiting illegitimacy. Following similar reasoning, the Court has rejected a statute relegating unacknowledged illegitimate children to a lower priority than legitimate children in recovering for the death of their natural parents under the state workmen's compensation program.[31] In this last case, the Court expressed its view in the following words:

> The status of illegitimacy has expressed through the ages society's condemnation of irresponsible liaisons beyond the bonds of marriage. But visiting this condemnation on the head of an infant is illogical and unjust. Moreover, imposing disabilities on the illegitimate child is contrary to the basic concept of our system that legal burdens should bear some relationship to individual responsibility or wrongdoing. Obviously, no child is responsible for his birth and penalizing the illegitimate child is an ineffectual — as well as unjust — way of deterring the parent.[32]

In the cases we have reviewed, the Court has established the principle that government cannot constitutionally punish illegitimate children simply because of their illegitimacy or because of a desire to induce couples not to have illegitimate progeny.[33] This principle also seems to be the basis for another set of opinions in which the issue was the right of illegitimate children to obtain certain benefits. In one case, the state common law gave legitimate, but not illegitimate, children the right to financial support from their natural (biological) fathers.[34] In a second case a state welfare program was operated in such a manner as to deny financial assistance and other services to illegitimate children while providing them to legitimate children.[35] In both cases the Court invoked the equal protection clause to invalidate discrimination against illegitimate children. In a third case the Court upheld a complex provision of the Social Security Act under which illegitimacy was employed simply as a reasonable, but not as an exclusive or conclusive, indicator of the likelihood of dependency upon a deceased parent and hence of eligibility to obtain benefits.[36] In these three cases the Court gave illegitimate children the right to receive necessary support from others when the same support had been given to legitimate children; the Court also gave government the right to utilize illegitimacy in a reasonable manner as an objective indicator of another, but permissible, criterion for the dispensation of benefits. In so doing, the Court appears to have expressed the philosophy that children cannot be penalized simply because they are illegitimate or because the government wants to reduce illegitimacy. The Court thus views children as possessing certain rights that are unaffected by the technical nature of their lineage — a view that reflects a reluctance to permit intrusions into the parent-child relationship.

In conclusion, we should note that the preceding cases do not permit one to determine the validity of government action designed to discourage illegitimacy that imposes a burden directly on parents. Could Congress, for instance, eliminate or substantially reduce retirement benefits under the Social Security Act to covered workers who have had one or more illegitimate children? If the measure reduced illegitimacy, it would do so in a manner that did not directly or seriously affect the children involved. Unfortunately, in cases where the Court has considered sanctions designed to discourage illegitimacy, the sanctions have fallen on the children. Even so, there is a strong indication that government would be required to satisfy the compelling interest test if it acted to discourage illegitimacy by imposing a penalty on the parents, because any such action would evidently be considered a serious intrusion on the right of privacy. In holding that Congress is not constitutionally required to provide public funds for abortions, the Court noted:

> A substantial constitutional question would arise if Congress had attempted to withhold all Medicaid benefits from an otherwise eligible candidate simply because that candidate had exercised her constitutionally protected freedom to terminate her pregnancy by abortion. This would be analogous to *Sherbert v Verner*, where this Court held that a State may not ... withhold *all* unemployment compensation benefits from a claimant who would otherwise be eligible for such benefits but for the fact that she is unwilling to work one day per week on her Sabbath.[37]

Any withdrawal of government benefits from the parents of illegitimate children that was designed to induce unmarried persons not to have children would seem to fall under this principle. The Court protects abortion and childbearing equally under the right of privacy and would probably find penalties that might be imposed for having an illegitimate child as objectionable as penalties imposed for having an abortion. Given the apparent violation of the right of privacy by sanctions against the parents, government would be forced to meet the compelling interest standard. One might argue that the reduction of illegitimacy is a compelling governmental interest because illegitimate infants evidently suffer higher death rates than their legitimate counterparts of the same economic status.[38] If a sanction devised along these lines were the narrowest possible, it might be held constitutionally valid. However, the important point is that the Constitution has provided unmarried parents with an umbrella that minimizes the opportunities for government to place burdens on them and has thereby allowed the incidence of illegitimacy to be higher than it might otherwise be.

### Educational Costs

Since the Court has expressly stated that the primary obligation for the rearing of children resides in the parents, we are correct in anticipating that imposing the financial costs of education on parents has not generally given rise to constitutional concerns. The Court has long recognized the importance of education in the preparation of children for adult life,[39] and it has indicated that government can require parents to send their children to school for a minimum number of years.[40] At the same time the Court has held that the parent-child relationship is protected to the extent that parents can choose to send their children to private schools,[41] and they can exempt their children from a short period of required formal schooling if they are doing so because of a genuine religious belief and are providing alternate education of equivalent utility.[42] These decisions reflect the philosophy that parents have primary control over, and responsibility for, the upbringing of their children; that government cannot intrude on the parent-child relationship unless it possesses a sufficiently important purpose, such as assuring an education adequate for acquiring the essential skills needed by children to function as adults;[43] and that parents have the right and the duty to determine the most suitable location for the education of their children as long as reasonable governmental standards are satisfied.[44]

Given the Court's recognition of the importance of education for children and given the responsibility of parents to provide such education, the question arises whether government is constitutionally compelled to offer educational services at public expense. The answer is negative. The Court has pointed out that the Constitution does not explicitly guarantee a right to education, and it has further held that no implicit right to education exists.[45] However, the Court has also indicated that if government offered educational services for which a tuition charge was imposed that absolutely precluded financially impoverished children from obtaining an education, the poor would constitute a suspect class under the equal protection clause, and judicial intervention would then be likely.[46]

It should be kept in mind that tuition charges in private schools— to which parents have a constitutional right to send their children— are permissible and, indeed, necessary to the operation of the schools. The question of private school tuition has led to a relevant line of case law. In order to alleviate the costs to parents of sending their children to private schools, state and local governments have attempted to develop programs of financial aid to nonpublic education, but the programs have been challenged under the establishment clause of the First Amendment, which prohibits a "law respecting an establishment of religion," because most private schools are affiliated with religious groups.[47] As a general standard, the Court has said that such programs are permissible if they have a secular purpose, if their principal effect neither advances nor hinders religion, and if they do not foster substantial entanglement between government and church.[48] Accordingly, the Court has upheld programs in which parents were reimbursed for the cost of transportation of their children to schools, both public and private, by public buses[49] and in which public school textbooks on secular subjects were loaned free of charge to students in private schools.[50] On the other hand, the Court has invalidated a program through which parents were reimbursed up to designated amounts for private school tuition; the Court felt that the effect was to advance religion.[51] Another program that paid a part of the salaries of teachers of secular subjects in religious schools was struck down because the Court believed that excessive entanglements would develop from the government surveillance necessary to ensure that the teachers did not provide religious training. Also, the Court opined that political divisiveness would be likely along religious lines over the continuation and level of funding for the program.[52] The Court has also prohibited government from reimbursing religious schools for the costs of record keeping and of teacher-prepared tests, even though the costs resulted from government-imposed requirements.[53] The Court has, therefore, placed severe restrictions on the flow of public funds into private religious schools. In striking down a program for reimbursing low-income parents for a portion of private school tuition and giving middle-income parents a deduction for such tuition under the state income tax, the Court expressed the view that the financial burden placed on parents who chose to send their children to religious schools was a price to be paid for the advantages accompanying the separation of church and state mandated by the establishment clause.[54] Thus, the Court found, public funds used for direct or indirect payment of religious school tuition were not in the same category as reimbursement of the cost of bus transportation or provision of free textbooks for children attending private schools. The Court expressed its opinion as follows:

> We do not agree ... that tuition grants [or tax deductions for tuition] are an analogous endeavor to provide comparable benefits to all parents of school

children whether enrolled in public or nonpublic schools. The grants [and tax deductions] to parents of private schoolchildren are given in addition to the right that they have to send their children to public schools totally at state expense. And in any event, the argument proves too much, for it would also prove a basis for approving through tuition grants the complete subsidization of all religious schools on the ground that such action is necessary if the State is fully to equalize the position of parents who elect such schools—a result wholly at variance with the Establishment Clause.[55]

To recapitulate, American constitutional philosophy has erected a barrier to governmental intrusion into the parent-child relationship and has placed on parents the principal responsibility of childrearing. In so doing, the Court has provided considerable protection for illegitimate children and at the same time has permitted educational costs to be placed on parents. Thus, the opportunity to exploit resources in the public domain varies between areas of constitutional philosophy relevant to the burdens of childbearing and childrearing.

## CHILDREARING AND SEX ROLES

Let us turn to another aspect of childrearing in American society in which exploitation of the public domain can exist. A widely accepted social philosophy—a commons—assigns to men and women roles under which children are generally expected to be (and in fact are) reared by women rather than by men. Child care duties and the career restrictions accompanying them have traditionally been defined as the responsibility of females rather than of both parents equally or of the parent with the most interest in and talent for the task. American men are therefore able to achieve a status—parenthood—that society deems desirable,[56] but women who become parents undertake the burdens of caring for the children and the home. That childrearing is a burden is suggested by the fact that the role of childrearer and housekeeper is generally considered relatively low in prestige[57] and is apparently responsible for higher rates of poor mental and physical health among women.[58] In assigning the childrearing role, then, American society places certain disadvantages on women and allows men to acquire a benefit at women's expense. Not surprisingly, men are more likely than women to consider parenthood an advantageous lifestyle.[59]

## Attitudes of Young Adults

A national study of high school seniors in the spring of 1977 provided recent empirical evidence on social expectations regarding the division of labor by sex for young adults who would shortly be entering their prime childbearing years.[60] The study examined the students' attitudes toward various arrangements for paid employment for husbands and wives in terms of married couples with no children and married couples with preschool children. For example, the students were asked to indicate whether they considered it "not acceptable," "somewhat acceptable," "acceptable," or "desirable" for both a husband and wife to work full-time when they had no children and when they had preschool children. The study also examined attitudes toward different arrangements for the care of preschool children after working hours and on weekends in the case of married couples where both husband and wife needed to work full-time. The students' attitudes with regard to the employment of both husband and wife were as follows:

1. There was a substantial increase in the proportion of students who viewed nonemployment for a wife as desirable when a couple changed from a state of childlessness to a state of parenthood. Only 9 percent of the students thought it desirable for a husband to work full-time and a wife not to work at all when a couple had no children, but 41 percent took this view when a couple had preschool children—a rise of 32 percentage points.
2. There was a dramatic increase in the proportion of students who considered it unacceptable for both spouses to be employed full-time when a couple changed from childlessness to parenthood. With the change, the proportion of students who found full-time employment of both husband and wife to be unacceptable increased from roughly two out of ten to seven out of ten—a rise of some 50 percentage points.

3. The increase in unfavorable attitudes was not so large in the case of a wife who worked part-time when she and her husband changed from childlessness to parenthood. In this case, 4 percent viewed an arrangement where a husband worked full-time and a wife worked part-time as unacceptable when a couple had no children, and 18 percent considered it unacceptable when a couple had preschool children—a rise of 14 percentage points.
4. Attitudes toward an arrangement in which both spouses worked half-time were not generally positive either in the case of nonparents or of parents. The same is true of attitudes toward the situation where a husband is employed half-time or not at all while a wife is employed full-time. A major change in, or a reversal of, sex roles was thus viewed with considerable disfavor.
5. The attitudes of male and female students were similar but not identical. Females were more inclined than males to accept employment by a wife even when she had preschool children.

When both spouses are employed full-time and arrangements need to be made for the care of children after working hours and on weekends, the students' attitudes were as follows:

1. An equal sharing of the burdens of child care was the arrangement thought most desirable. Nonetheless, the arrangement was considered desirable by only two out of five students.
2. The students considered it more acceptable for a wife to undertake responsibility for most or all of the child care than for a husband to do so. For example, 60 percent of the students found it unacceptable for a husband to do most of the child care, but only 33 percent found it unacceptable for a wife to do so. Roughly twice as many students thus felt it was unacceptable for a husband to carry the major part of child care duties as felt it was unacceptable for a wife. A comparable difference, though not quite as large, existed in attitudes toward males' and females' shouldering all child care obligations.
3. Male and female students had generally similar attitudes toward child care responsibilities. The differences that appeared

suggested that females were more oriented than males toward an equal sharing of child care duties.

These data suggest that young adults in the United States are even today quite conventional in their attitudes toward a division of labor by sex and that males and females are generally characterized by similar attitudes.[61] Women are expected to leave their jobs when children arrive, but males are expected to continue to pursue their careers. Furthermore, while a sharing of responsibility for preschool children is considered desirable when both spouses must be employed full-time, there remains a strong preference for wives to carry the major portion of this responsibility. Other evidence indicates that the preferences described are manifested in actual behavior and that there has been little change over the last several decades in the assignment of most child care duties to women.[62]

## Court Opinions

The manner in which American society defines the roles of males and females can be determined from court opinions involving constitutional issues as well as from survey research. In construing the Constitution, the judiciary tends to reflect current social ideals, and a review of court opinions indicates that it has manifested the changing ideals—though not necessarily the practices—of society with regard to sex roles. The Supreme Court today looks with disfavor on government action based upon traditional definitions of sex roles. The Court has labeled such action "part of the baggage of sexual stereotypes that presumes the father has the primary responsibility to provide a home and its essentials, while the mother is the center of home and family life."[63] The Court did not, however, arrive at this view until recently. In 1908 the Court upheld a state statute limiting the number of hours that women (but not men) could work each day in factories and laundries. The Court reasoned that the "disposition and habits" of women were such as to preclude equality with men and thus necessitated protective legislation for women. It expressed its view in the following words:

Even though all restrictions on [a woman's] political, personal, and contractual rights were taken away, and she stood, as far as statutes are concerned, upon an absolutely equal plane with [a man], it would still be true that she is so constituted that she will rest upon and look to him for protection; that her physical structure and a proper discharge of her maternal functions—having in view not merely her own health, but the well-being of the race—justify legislation to protect her from the greed as well as the passion of men.[64]

By the end of the 1970s, the Court had abandoned the view that women were inherently unequal to men. The Court gave constitutional blessing to legislation that provided an economic benefit to women as compensation for their disadvantageous position in the job market,[65] but it recognized that women's position was the result of past conditions that should be eliminated.[66] With regard to children, the Court noted that women were more likely than men to be responsible for child care,[67] but it expressly distinguished statistical reality from constitutional imperative.[68] The Court accepted the view that the individual should be free to choose or reject the childrearing role and that government action based on stereotyped sex roles raised serious constitutional questions. Accordingly, in *Weinberger v Wiesenfeld* the Court invalidated a provision of the Social Security Act under which benefits were payable to both the wife and the children of a deceased man but only to the children (and not to the husband) of a deceased woman. In holding that the provision violated the guarantee of equal protection, the Court pointed out that the purpose of the act was to permit the surviving parent to stay at home and care for the child(ren) and that a legislative assumption that a surviving mother, but not a surviving father, would want to do so was not constitutionally valid. The Court reasoned as follows:

> The fact that a man is working while there is a wife at home does not mean that he would, or should be required to, continue to work if his wife dies. It is no less important for a child to be cared for by its sole surviving parent when that parent is male rather than female. And a father, no less than a mother, has a constitutionally protected right to the companionship, care, custody, and management of the children he has sired and raised, [which] undeniably warrants deference and, absent a powerful countervailing interest, protection.[69]

\* \* \*

In summary, current constitutional philosophy places major obstacles in the way of government action that presumes individuals will adopt social roles consistent with traditional conceptions of family life. Judicial opinion also discourages government from establishing impediments to the adoption of roles inconsistent with traditional sex roles.[70] Constitutional philosophy thus seems to express an ideal that is apparently ahead of current social practice, for as we have seen, young adults still favor a traditional division of labor by sex with regard to family life. Whether Americans will abandon this view and allow individuals to make career and child-rearing decisions freely and without social pressure remains to be seen. If such a situation develops, men will be faced with assuming an equal share of the burdens of the childrearing role in order to achieve the status of parenthood, while women will be free to reject the burdens. The likely result will be a lowered birth rate.[71]

## NOTES

1. Garrett J. Hardin, *The Tragedy of the Commons,* in Managing the Commons 16, 20 (Garrett J. Hardin & John Baden, eds.; San Francisco: W.H. Freeman, 1977).

In 1976 Congress enacted legislation that extended the exclusive fisheries zone of the United States from 12 to 200 miles from the coast and required the development of regulations to govern fishing within the zone. The need for legislation was explained as follows by a committee of the House of Representatives:

> [T]he high rate of foreign fishing, the old age of [American] vessels and crewmen, and the low earnings to labor and capital in certain fisheries are primary symptoms rather than causes. That is, these are characteristic of a common property resource in which there is no ownership of the resource and thus entry (either by foreign or domestic interests) into the fishery takes place as long as there is economic rent or profit to be earned. This means that in any fishery, unless there are restrictions on entry, fishing effort tends to increase to a level where average profits — or economic rent attributable to the resource — is dissipated.

House Merchant Marine & Fisheries Committee, Fishery Conservation and Management Act of 1976, H.R. Rep. No. 445, 94th Cong., 2d Sess. 30, *reprinted in* [1976] U.S. Code Congressional & Administrative News 593, 602-3.

2. James Acheson, *The Lobster Fiefs: Economic and Ecological Effects of Territoriality in the Maine Lobster Industry,* 3 Human Ecology 183 (1975).

3. Robert Cass & Julian Edney, *The Commons Dilemma: A Simulation Testing the Effects of Resource Visibility and Territorial Division,* 6 Human Ecology 371 (1978).

4. Julian Edney & Christopher Harper, *The Effects of Information in a Resource Management Problem: A Social Trap Analog,* 6 Human Ecology 387 (1978).

5. Julian Edney & Christopher Harper, *Heroism in a Resource Crisis: A Simulation Study,* 2 Environmental Management 523 (1978). *See* Julian Edney & Christopher Harper, *The Commons Dilemma: A Review of Contributions from Psychology,* 2 Environmental Management 491 (1978).

6. John W. Sweeney, Jr., *An Experimental Investigation of the Free-Rider Problem,* 2 Social Science Research 277 (1973); Paul Gump, *Big Schools-Small Schools,* in Issues in Social Ecology 276 (Rudolf H. Moos & Paul M. Insel, eds.; Palo Alto, Calif.: National Press Books, 1974); Allan Wicker, *Size of Church Membership and Members' Support of Church Behavior Settings,* in *id.* at 286; Julian Edney & Christopher Harper, *The Commons Dilemma: A Review of Contributions from Psychology,* 2 Environmental Management 491 (1978).

7. Rodolfo Bulatao & Fred Arnold, *Relationships Between the Value and Cost of Children and Fertility: Cross-Cultural Evidence,* in 1 International Population Conference, Mexico, 1977 141, 146 (International Union for the Scientific Study of Population, 1977); Rodolfo Bulatao, *Values and Disvalues of Children in Successive Childbearing Decisions,* 18 Demography 1 (1981); "Attitudes about Children: Report to Respondents" (Survey Research Center, Institute for Social Research, University of Michigan, October 1976), at table 2.

8. Bureau of the Census, U.S. Department of Commerce, Statistical Abstract of the United States: 1980, 101st ed., 162 (Washingon, D.C.: U.S. Gov't. Printing Office, 1980).

9. I.R.C. § 44A. The tax credit is 20 percent of child care expenses that are incurred, with a maximum of $2,000 for one dependent child under fifteen years of age and a maximum of $4,000 for two or more dependent children. It should be noted that this is a tax credit, not a deduction. A tax credit is subtracted from taxes owed, while a deduction only reduces the income subject to taxation. A tax credit is thus a more direct financial benefit. However, under the current Internal Revenue Code, parents also have a $1,000 deduction for each dependent child. I.R.C. § 151(e), 152(a).

10. *See* references in note 7, *supra.*

11. John Boli-Bennett & John Meyer, *The Ideology of Childhood and the State: Rules Distinguishing Children in National Constitutions, 1870-1970,* 43 American Sociological Review 797 (1978).

12. *Id.* at 810.

13. *Id.* at 801.

14. In order to maximize the comparability of the review of constitutional interpretation with the research by Boli-Bennett and Meyer on national constitutions, cases decided by the U.S. Supreme Court will be the sole focus. It is the

only court that can interpret the Constitution definitively for the nation as a whole.

15. Quilloin v Walcott, 434 U.S. 246, 255 (1978) [quoting from Prince v Massachusetts, 321 U.S. 158, 166 (1944)]. *See* Meyer v Nebraska, 262 U.S. 390, 399-400 (1923).

16. Bureau of the Census, *supra* note 8, at 66. In 1978 there were approximately 543,900 births to unmarried women.

17. Roe v Wade, 410 U.S. 113 (1973).

18. Stanley Henshaw, Jacqueline Forrest, Ellen Sullivan, & Christopher Tietze, *Abortion in the United States, 1978-1979*, 13 Family Planning Perspectives 6 (1981); Jacqueline Forrest, Ellen Sullivan, & Christopher Tietze, *Abortion in the United States, 1977-1978*, 11 Family Planning Perspectives 329 (1979).

19. *See* Larry Freshnock & Phillips Cutright, *Models of Illegitimacy: United States, 1969*, 16 Demography 37 (1979).

20. The Fourteenth Amendment provides that "[n]o State shall . . . deny to any person within its jurisdiction the equal protection of the laws" and thus places restrictions on classifications. There is no express guarantee of equal protection applicable to the federal government, but one has been inferred from the due process clause of the Fifth Amendment. Hampton v Wong, 426 U.S. 88 (1976). See note 22 *infra*.

21. Carey v Population Services Int'l, 431 U.S. 678, 685 (1977).

22. *Id.*
Under the due process clauses, government may not deprive a person of "life, liberty or property, without due process of law." The clauses are found in the Fifth and Fourteenth Amendments, the former applying to the federal government and the latter to states.

23. Dandridge v Williams, 397 U.S. 471 (1970); Roe v Wade, *supra* note 17. See Note, *Of Interests, Fundamental and Compelling: The Emerging Constitutional Balance*, 57 Boston University Law Review 462 (1977).

24. Zablocki v Redhail, 434 U.S. 374, 387 (1978).

25. San Antonio Ind. School Dist. v Rodriguez, 411 U.S. 1, 28 (1973).

26. Weber v Aetna Casualty & Surety Co., 406 U.S. 164, 172 (1972).

27. Eisenstadt v Baird, 405 U.S. 438, 453 (1972); Carey v Population Services Int'l, *supra* note 21.

28. Mathews v Lucas, 427 U.S. 495, 504-6 (1976); Lalli v Lalli, 439 U.S. 259, 273 (1978).

29. Levy v Louisiana, 391 U.S. 68, 72 (1968).

30. Glona v American Guarantee & Liability Ins. Co., 391 U.S. 73, 75 (1968).

31. Weber v Aetna Casualty & Surety Co., *supra* note 26, at 173.

32. *Id.* at 175.

33. See also Trimble v Gordon, 430 U.S. 762, 769 (1977).

34. Gomez v Perez, 409 U.S. 535 (1973).

35. New Jersey Welfare Rights Organization v Cahill, 411 U.S. 619 (1973).

36. Mathews v Lucas, *supra* note 28.

37. Harris v McRae, 100 S.Ct. 2671, 2688 n.19 (1980).
38. Beth Berkov & June Sklar, *Does Illegitimacy Make a Difference? A Study of the Life Chances of Illegitimate Children in California,* 2 Population & Development Review 201 (1976).
39. *E.g.,* Brown v Bd. of Educ., 347 U.S. 483, 493 (1954).
40. Lemon v Kurtzman, 403 U.S. 602, 614 (1971); Wisconsin v Yoder, 406 U.S. 205, 213 (1972).
41. Pierce v Society of Sisters, 268 U.S. 510 (1925).
42. Wisconsin v Yoder, 406 U.S. 205 (1972).
43. In Wisconsin v Yoder, the Court notes: "The history and culture of Western civilization reflect a strong tradition of parental concern for the nurture and upbringing of their children. This primary role of the parents in the upbringing of their children is now established beyond debate as an enduring American tradition." *Id.* at 232.
44. In Meyer v Nebraska, *supra* note 15, at 400, the Court states: "Corresponding to the right of control, it is the natural duty of the parent to give his children education suitable to their station in life . . . ."
45. San Antonio Ind. School Dist. v Rodriguez, *supra* note 25, at 35.
46. *Id.* at 25 n.60.
The question of charging parents for the education of their children in the public schools is discussed at greater length in chapter 9.
47. Of all students attending nonpublic schools in 1978, 94 percent of those in elementary schools and 91 percent of those in secondary schools were attending institutions that were religiously affiliated. *See* Bureau of the Census, *supra* note 8, at 155.
48. Lemon v Kurtzman, *supra* note 40, at 612-13.
49. Everson v Bd. of Educ., 330 U.S. 1 (1947).
50. Bd. of Educ. v Allen, 392 U.S. 236 (1968). *See also* Cochran v Louisiana State Bd. of Educ., 281 U.S. 370 (1930), Norwood v Harrison, 413 U.S. 455 (1973). However, the Court has invalidated a program for the loan of instructional materials and equipment—for example, periodicals, maps, and films. The materials and equipment were adaptable to a wide variety of uses within the teaching process, which in church-related schools includes religious training. Meek v Pittenger, 421 U.S. 349 (1975).
51. Sloan v Lemon, 413 U.S. 825 (1973).
52. Lemon v Kurtzman, *supra* note 40.
53. Levitt v Comm. for Pub. Educ., 413 U.S. 472 (1973). However, public funds may be used to provide state-prepared tests on secular subjects to nonpublic schools and to reimburse such schools for the costs of administering and grading the tests as long as adequate safeguards exist to prevent use of the funds for religious instruction. Wolman v Walter, 433 U.S. 229 (1977); Comm. for Pub. Educ. v Regan, 100 S.Ct. 840 (1980).
54. Comm. for Pub. Educ. v Nyquist, 413 U.S. 756 (1973).
55. *Id.* at 782 n.38.
56. Judith Blake, *Is Zero Preferred? American Attitudes toward Childlessness in the 1970s,* 41 Journal of Marriage & the Family 245 (1979); Denise

Polit, *Stereotypes Relating to Family-Size Status,* 40 Journal of Marriage & the Family 105 (1978).

57. Lucille Duberman, Social Inequality 287 (Philadelphia: Lippincott, 1976); Cynthia Epstein, *Women's Place: Options and Limits in Professional Careers,* in Issues in Social Inequality 597 (Gerald Thielbar & Saul Feldman eds.; Boston: Little, Brown, 1972); Anne Macke, George Bohrnstedt, & Ilene Bernstein, *Housewives' Self-Esteem and Their Husbands' Success: The Myth of Vicarious Involvement,* 41 Journal of Marriage & the Family 51 (1979).

58. Walter Gove & Michael Hughes, *Possible Causes of the Apparent Sex Differences in Physical Health: An Empirical Investigation,* 44 American Sociological Review 126 (1979); Walter Gove & Michael Geerken, *The Effect of Children and Employment on the Mental Health of Married Men and Women,* 56 Social Forces 66 (1977).

59. Blake, *supra* note 56, at 255.

60. A. Regula Herzog, Jerald Bachman, & Lloyd Johnston, "High School Seniors' Preferences for Sharing Work and Family Responsibilities Between Husband and Wife" (Survey Research Center, Institute for Social Research, University of Michigan, 1978), table 3.

61. That women generally support the traditional sex role assignments does not eliminate the exploitation problem. A commons — here, the philosophy for distributing sex roles — characterized by exploitation would appear as a rule to exist through explicit or implicit agreement.

62. Stan Albrecht, Howard Bahr, & Bruce Chadwick, *Changing Family and Sex Roles: An Assessment of Age Differences,* 41 Journal of Marriage & the Family 41 (1979). *See* Wendy Wolf & Rachel Rosenfeld, *Sex Structure of Occupations and Job Mobility,* 56 Social Forces 823 (1978).

63. Califano v Westcott, 443 U.S. 76, 89 (1979).

64. Muller v Oregon, 208 U.S. 412, 422 (1908).

65. Kahn v Shevin, 416 U.S. 351 (1974); Califano v Webster, 430 U.S. 313 (1977).

66. Stanton v Stanton, 421 U.S. 7, 14-15 (1975).

67. "No longer is the female destined *solely* for the home and the rearing of the family, and only the male for the marketplace and the world of ideas" (italics added). *Id.* at 14-15. *Accord,* Weinberger v Wiesenfeld, 420 U.S. 636, 645 (1975). *See* Taylor v Louisiana, 419 U.S. 522, 537 (1975).

68. Craig v Boren, 429 U.S. 190, 204 (1976).

69. Weinberger v Wiesenfeld, *supra* note 67, at 651-52.

70. *See* White v Fleming, 522 F.2d 730, 737, (7th Cir. 1975), which states: "There are anatomical and physiological differences between the sexes that may justify classification for certain purposes. But these differences hardly include a greater or lesser propensity for a given kind of conduct."

71. *See* John Scanzoni, *Gender Roles and the Process of Fertility Control,* 38 Journal of Marriage & the Family 677 (1976); Alice Eagly & Pamela Anderson, *Sex Role and Attitudinal Correlates of Desired Family Size,* 4 Journal of Applied Social Psychology 151 (1974).

# 5 LEGAL PROTECTION AND FEMALE EMPLOYMENT

Population policymakers have argued for many years that the elimination of sex discrimination in employment is a desirable, if not essential, prerequisite to the attainment of a sustained low level of fertility. With the abolition of sex descrimination, they contend, commitment to careers will increase among women and family size will fall. In 1972 the U.S. Commission on Population Growth and the American Future concluded:

> [W]e believe that attractive work may effectively compete with childbearing and have the effect of lowering fertility, especially higher-order births. Virtually all American couples want at least one child, but there is some evidence that rewarding employment may compete successfully with childbearing beyond the first child.[1]

Recent social science research, however, has cast serious doubt on the proposition that the employment of women reduces fertility. Some studies have indicated that employment does not affect childbearing at all and that any fertility difference found between women who work and women who do not is attributable to factors other than work status.[2] Other research, constituting a more substantial body of evidence, has found that a relationship does exist between childbearing and female employment, but the net causal connection runs in the opposite direction from what population policymakers believe. This research indicates that childbearing decisions are the determining factors in the extent of participation of women in the labor force; higher family-size preferences and fertility reduce the incidence of female employment.[3] "In other words," one such study concluded, "the number of children a women has may influence her work decisions, but her labor force involvement does not alter her fertility behavior."[4] It thus appears that, contrary to the argument that employment determines and controls fertility, women consider childbearing decisions to be more important than employment.[5]

The relationship between fertility and employment is important to population policy. If family size is the antecedent rather than the effect of employment of women, legal protections for women in the job market can promote fertility by making it easier for women to have children, because childbearing can be undertaken without deleterious consequences in regard to job opportunities and income. Research has shown that the financial factor is a dominant constraint on decisions about family size[6] and a principal inducement for wives to enter the labor force;[7] thus, the cost of children limits family size while simultaneously motivating women to work. Since 1973 the increasing price of oil has caused rapid rises in the cost of all items, including the cost of raising children. Because of the lower productivity accompanying higher fossil fuel prices, the cost of oil has also caused relatively slow growth in wages.[8] The result has been strong financial incentives for women to work and supplement their family incomes.[9] If the legal system expands employment opportunities for women, people will find it financially easier to maintain a desired level of fertility and thus such fertility will be more likely.[10] As one female demographer has noted, women's liberation and population control may have divergent concerns.[11]

## CONGRESSIONAL POWERS OVER SEX DISCRIMINATION

At least two constitutional provisions—the commerce clause and the equal protection clause—can be utilized to prohibit sex discrimination in employment, but to understand the nature and operation of these constitutional safeguards, we must make a distinction between discrimination by private entities and discrimination by government agencies. A further distinction must be made between the ability of the judiciary to employ the Constitution directly to invalidate discriminatory conduct — that is, to strike down such conduct under the Constitution without reliance on a federal statute — and the ability of Congress to enact legislation to suppress discriminatory conduct. Table 5.1 shows the relationship between the two sets of distinctions and indicates when each branch of the federal government can suppress sex discrimination in employment. Let us examine the constitutional basis of each cell in the table. It is virtually certain that Congress can prohibit sex discrimination by private employers through statutes enacted under its power to regulate interstate commerce.[12] Such statutes have already been adopted,[13] and while their constitutionality has not been definitively decided by the courts, there is little doubt that they are valid.[14] Congress has broad powers to control that which affects national commerce: "Even activity that is purely intrastate in character may be regulated by Congress where the activity, combined with like conduct by others similarly situated, affects commerce among the States or with foreign nations."[15] To the extent that sex discrimination exists and causes women to earn less than men, purchasing power is lowered and the national economy is affected, thus allowing Congress to ban discrimination.

While the power to regulate interstate commerce provides Congress with the constitutional authority to prohibit sex discrimination in the private sector, it may not allow such a prohibition to be applied to state governments.[16] The guarantee of equal protection,

Table 5.1  Remedies for Discrimination by Private and Government Agencies

| Source of Discrimination | Statute Enacted by Congress | Constitution Applied by Judiciary |
|---|---|---|
| Private organizations | Yes | No |
| Government agencies | Yes | Yes |

however, expressly authorizes Congress to forbid state and local governments from classifying people into groups and treating groups in different ways.[17] The courts, citing the authority given Congress to enforce the equal protection guarantee, have consistently upheld legislation prohibiting state and local governments from classification and differential treatment of employees on the basis of gender.[18]

No constitutional provision, it should be noted, empowers Congress to legislate enforcement of equal protection for agencies of the federal government.[19] However, Congress is apparently able to prohibit sex discrimination in federal employment through its power to regulate the incidents of interstate commerce as well as through its power to promote the general welfare in the expenditure of tax revenues (in this case, employee salaries).[20] Indeed, a statute forbidding pay differences based on sex already exists.[21]

## JUDICIAL POWERS OVER SEX DISCRIMINATION

In turning our attention to use of the Constitution by the judiciary to prevent sex discrimination, we are concerned with situations in which sex discrimination exists but to which no legislation is applicable. The question to be examined is the conditions under which the courts can employ the Constitution to suppress discrimination. The constitutional provision that has been applied to date is the equal protection guarantee, whose scope includes both "equality of treatment" and "treatment as an equal":

> The *right to equal treatment* holds with respect to a limited set of interests — like voting — and demands that every person have the same access to these interests as every other person. Note that this right to equal treatment clearly does not operate with respect to all interests; any such universal demand for sameness would prevent government from discriminating in the public interest. On the other hand, the *right to treatment as an equal* holds with regard to all interests and requires government to treat each individual with equal regard as a person. This is not to say that every political outcome which operates to an individual's disadvantage should be deemed to deny treatment as an equal, but only to single out for special scrutiny and probable invalidation those disadvantageous political judgments which seem likely to reflect a preference based on prejudice.[22]

## State Action and the Equal Protection Clause

Although applicable to the federal as well as to the state and local level,[23] the equal protection guarantee provides the judiciary with the authority only to ban action by government.[24] Sex discrimination in the private sector is beyond the reach of the guarantee unless the existence of government action—usually labelled generically "state action"—can be found. State action exists in the conduct of officers, employees, and agencies of government, but it can also exist in the conduct of an ostensibly private entity that is performing a traditional, exclusively governmental function or that is significantly involved with government.[25] The conditions necessary for attributing state action to the conduct of a private entity can vary with the nature of the alleged constitutional violation; what will constitute state action for one type of injury may not do so for another. Under the equal protection clause of the Fourteenth Amendment, which was adopted primarily to eliminate discrimination against blacks,[26] courts have been more willing to find state action in cases where race discrimination has been alleged than in cases involving other types of alleged discrimination.[27] How has the state action issue been treated in cases involving complaints of sex bias brought under the equal protection clause?[28] Our review will focus on the treatment of the issue by the judiciary when sex discrimination has allegedly occurred in employment and in related fields.[29]

*Weise v Syracuse University.* The U.S. Court of Appeals for the Second Circuit (which covers Connecticut, New York, and Vermont) has held that it will employ a lower threshold for finding state action in cases of sex discrimination. The lower threshold emerged in 1975 in *Weise v Syracuse University.*[30] Plaintiffs were two females who alleged that the defendant university injured them by favoring less qualified males in employment. One plaintiff had been rejected for a teaching position in favor of a male but later was hired as a teaching assistant. The second plaintiff had been employed in a full-time, tenure-track teaching position at the university but was denied tenure and terminated; at the same time two male colleagues were granted tenure and a male colleague who had also been turned down for tenure was granted an extension of his teaching contract. Suit was filed under 42 U.S.C. § 1983, which prohibits the violation of an individual's constitutional rights "under color of any statute, ordinance, regulation, custom, or usage of any State."[31] The statutory requirement of "under color of" law appears equivalent here to the state action requirement of the Fourteenth Amendment,[32] and the court treated it as such.[33]

In deciding on the standard to use for state action, *Weise* begins with the premise that there must be a balancing of two factors. In the words of the court:

> As the conduct complained of becomes more offensive, and as the nature of the dispute becomes more amenable to resolution by a court, the more appropriate it is to subject the issue to judicial scrutiny. [The first factor] explains the willingness to find state action in racial discrimination cases although the same state-private relationship might not trigger such a finding in a case involving a different dispute over a different interest. Class-based discrimination is perhaps the practice most fundamentally opposed to the stuff of which our national heritage is composed, and by far the most evil form of discrimination has been that based on race. . . . Plaintiffs contend that we should put sex discrimination in the same category of offensiveness as race discrimination. We are not, however, engaged in an all-or-nothing, pigeonhole form of jurisprudence, and it is not necessary to put sex discrimination into the same hole as race discrimination to hold that in this case a less stringent state action standard should be employed [since there has allegedly been] invidious class-based discrimination on account of sex [and since] judicial resolution of this [employment termination] dispute will not entail interference with matters unsuited for review by a court.[34]

Because of an inadequate factual record, the court did not apply the lesser state action standard but, rather, returned the case to the trial court for a hearing. Unfortunately, there has been no subsequent hearing and opinion. However, since *Weise* one federal district court in the Second Circuit has faced two sex discrimination cases relevant to employment and has applied the lower state action standard. In the first case, plaintiff was a Caucasian female whose application to enter the law school of the defendant university was rejected while allegedly less qualified minority students were admitted under a special program.[35] Plaintiff claimed that a law degree from the defendant would facilitate her legal career; that the minority admissions policy discriminated on the basis of sex and race in violation of 42 U.S.C. § 1983; and that, though ostensibly a private institution, the defendant was engaged in conduct constituting state action. Using the less stringent standard indicated in *Weise,* the court rejected the argument that state action existed. The court based its decision on the following factors:[36]

1. Tax exemptions and funds provided the defendent by the state did not create a significant dependence of the defendant on the state.
2. Tax exemptions and funds from the state were not related to the existence of the minority admissions policy.
3. There was no apparent state regulation or control of the law school admissions policy.
4. The educational services provided by the defendant did not constitute the performance of a public function.
5. The minority admissions policy was not sufficiently offensive to the public interest to outweigh the defendant's claim to private status.

The court's inclusion of the last (fifth) factor is significant because it brings in the influence of public policy, a consideration going beyond the facts of the state–private entity relationship in a particular case. The court does not specify its reason(s) for reaching its conclusion; however, we should note that the minority admissions policy applied to roughly 10 percent of the entering class and that there was no discrimination against women in admissions decisions for 90 percent of the openings in the entering class. The policy merely reduced to a small extent the ability of Caucasian women to enter the law school; it did not totally preclude them from admission or even substantially affect their chances for admission. Thus, the court may have balanced the minimal reduction in opportunities for admission experienced by majority women against the importance of admission of minority persons and concluded that the latter had beneficial social consequences that were at least equal to the detrimental consequences of the former. If such was indeed the reasoning of the court, the public policy suggested by the decision is that a relatively minor constriction of opportunities for postbaccalaureate education of majority women is not an influential factor in determining the existence of state action under a less stringent standard when the constriction stems from an attempt to promote the education of other groups that have suffered discrimination. If such a counterweight to sex discrimination in a graduate school admissions policy did not exist, a substantial reason would presumably exist for finding state action under the less stringent standard. Moreover, the argument for state action would presumably be far stronger if a minority admissions policy applied to a large portion of the entering class and significantly reduced the opportunities for majority women to acquire a postbaccalaureate education.

*Ludke v Kuhn.* The same court has, since *Weise,* dealt with the issue of state action in a case involving sex discrimination relevant to employment. Plaintiff in the case of *Ludke v Kuhn* was a female reporter for a major sports magazine who was denied access, while male reporters were admitted, to the locker room of the New York Yankees baseball team following games played in Yankee Stadium.[37] She challenged the policy, which stemmed from action by the commissioner of baseball, under 42 U.S.C. § 1983 on the grounds that the exclusion policy severely hampered the ability of female sports reporters to gather information on baseball and its players. The court, applying the less stringent standard, found state action to exist in the Yankees team and in the stadium, which the team operated and in which the exclusion policy was enforced.[38] The court concluded that the team though it appeared to be a private entity, was heavily dependent on governmental aid. For instance, under a special state statute the City of New York owned the stadium and leased it to the Yankees rather than to the highest bidder. The city had also recently renovated the stadium at a cost of some $50 million. The court reasoned that the lease agreement, which provided that the rent paid by the Yankees would be proportional to attendance at the team's games played in the stadium, "recognizes the connection between publicity and increased attendance"[39] and thereby gives the city a direct stake in the rules imposed on reporters in the stadium. In addition to recognizing a financial relationship between the Yankees and the city, the court found it significant that the city had the authority to prohibit the exclusion of female reporters from stadium locker rooms but had failed to act even though it was apparently unsympathetic with the exclusion. Finally, probably based on the considerable public interest generated by sports events and the wide dissemination of material obtained by sports reporters, the court deemed the stadium to be devoted to public use.

In its analysis of the state action issue, the court also attempted to balance the interest of the Yankees in being a private entity against the public interest in prohibiting the challenged conduct.[40] Unfortunately, the opinion was not clearly written on this point. The court apparently found that the public interest in obtaining sports information from the most competent reporters and in eliminating class-based discrimination supported by tax revenues was not balanced by any countervailing interest of the Yankees. If the court did in fact reason in this way, the two opinions we have examined suggest that the several factors involved in a state action determination are consistent. That is, where one factor suggests the existence or nonexistence of state action, the other factors will point in the same direction. Nonetheless, the presence in the Second Circuit of the factor balancing public and private interests may prove important in a future case where other factors point toward no state action but where the balancing factor suggests otherwise and, under the lower state action threshold for sex discrimination, outweighs the others.

*Cases Involving Educational Institutions.* The lower state action threshold of the Second Circuit has not played a decisive role in court decisions to date. We now turn to an examination of how other circuits, which have not adopted a lower threshold, have handled the state action requirement. The following discussion is organized according to the type of entity that has allegedly discriminated.

Institutions of higher education have constituted the only frequent target in sex discrimination litigation in which the issue of state action has arisen. Five cases involving colleges and universities exist; four of the five were brought by discharged employees, and one was brought by an applicant who was denied admission to a university medical school. State action was found in only two of the five cases.[41] In both cases, which arose in the Third Circuit (Pennsylvania, Delaware, and New Jersey), the most important factor creating state action appears to have been the substantial financial dependence on the state of the ostensibly private universities. The state provided one-third of one institution's operating income and roughly one-tenth of the other's, and the court found that both institutions would face dire financial problems if state funding were eliminated. In addition, each of the two defendant universities had received state aid totaling tens of millions of dollars for construction of buildings and facilities.[42]

A second factor creating state action was the public control to which each institution was subjected with its acceptance of financial aid from the state. Particularly relevant to one case was that, pursuant to a state statute applicable explicitly to the institution, one-third of the members of the board of trustees of the institution were appointed by the governor and leaders of the state legislature, and additional trustees were on the board by virtue of their holding specified public offices, "thus seeming to ensure that governmental representation on the Board is rather substantial."[43] In the other case the court stressed that financial dependence on the state subjected the university to informal controls because it was doubtful "that the University would ever make major policy decisions without looking over its shoulder to gauge the attitude of its omnipresent informal partner."[44]

A third factor creating state action was the public nature acquired by each university. A state statute expressly changed the name of one of the institutions to reflect its incorporation into the state system of higher education and declared the university to be an "instrumentality" of the state. The other university had entered into agreements with a state agency whereby the university was able to purchase land that the agency, using the power of eminent domain, had acquired pursuant to the agreements. In addition, both universities gave preference in admissions and tuition charges to state residents and thereby provided a public service.[45]

In the three remaining cases involving sex discrimination by educational institutions, state action was not found. Two decisions from the U.S. Court of Appeals for the Seventh Circuit (which covers Illinois, Indiana, and Wisconsin) found no state action because the state evidently exercised no control over, and did not give its approval to, the policy or practice responsible for the alleged sex discrimination:[46]

[N]either general government involvement nor even extensive detailed state regulation is sufficient for a finding of state action. Rather, the state must affirmatively support and be directly involved in the specific conduct which is being challenged. . . . In this case, where there appears to be no state connection to the injury alleged, where there is no indication that the State exercises any control of the [challenged] policies, it would be improper to divest the . . . . schools of their private character.[47]

Under the Seventh Circuit approach, the indispensable ingredient for state action is control or approval by the state of the discriminatory policies of the ostensibly private entity. General regulation of the entity by the state, even as part of the receipt of state financial aid by the entity, is not sufficient for state action unless it can be said that the regulation controls or expressly condones the challenged policies. This requirement goes beyond the second factor for state action in the Third Circuit cases found on page 84. There, general regulation of the private entity was one, though not the most important, factor in finding state action, and there was no requirement, as in the Seventh Circuit, that the state regulation directly control or explicitly approve the challenged policies.[48]

The final case involving the state action issue in an institution of higher education comes from the U.S. Court of Appeals for the First Circuit (which covers Maine, Massachusetts, New Hampshire, Puerto Rico, and Rhode Island). In a suit against the Rhode Island School of Design for alleged sex discrimination, the court examined the contacts between the state and the defendant and found that the state provided funds amounting to roughly 1 percent of the defendant's operating budget; that the defendant, along with other educational institutions, was exempt from state taxes; that the city where the school was located had given the defendant a building about thirty years earlier; that a state agency had its offices in one of the defendant's buildings and another state agency had helped the defendant to obtain federal funds; that state law required the state commissioner of education to be one of the forty-three members of the defendant's board of directors; and that the defendant's by-laws required three other designated public officials to be board members.[49] However, these contacts, in the eyes of the court, were not adequate to create state action.

The First Circuit opinion suggested that, even under a less stringent standard, no state action would be found, because "the dependence of [defendant] on state aid is minuscule and there is no suggestion of the state's intrusion into hiring decisions."[50] Nonetheless, a strong argument can be made that state action could be found under a less stringent standard because of close ties between the defendant and the state. State statutes expressly naming the defendant authorized direct state funding for it and inspection of its facilities, required annual reports to be sent to the state by the defendant, required the state commissioner of education to serve on the defendant's board of directors, and provided funds for scholarships for students at the school.[51] Moreover, in creating the Rhode Island State Council on the Arts, a state statute declared it "to be the policy of the state to join with the federal government, private patrons, and institutions and professional organizations concerned with the arts to insure that the role of the arts in the life of Rhode Island communities will continue to grow and will play an ever more significant part in the welfare and educational experience of our citizens."[52] The offices of the council were located in one of the buildings on the campus of the defendant, and the council assisted the defendant in seeking state funds—facts that suggest the existence of a mutually beneficial relationship. Under a less stringent standard, there would seem to have been sufficient contacts with the state for a finding of state action.

*Additional Cases of Sex Discrimination.* Apart from institutions of higher education, only three cases exist in which state action was an issue in a claim of sex discrimination in employment. In one case no state action was found where the defendant was a food-manufacturing firm that was subjected to general health and other regulations by the state.[53] In a second case the defendant was a large bank in which deposits of state funds were held not to create state action.[54] State action was not found even though the defendant was extensively regulated by the state and there was financial interdependence between the state and the bank (e.g., the state was required by statute to deposit its money in banks, the state was authorized to appoint large banks as its fiscal agent for the payment of state bonds, and city retirement systems were authorized by statute to invest their funds in banks).[55] However, interdependence

LEGAL PROTECTION AND FEMALE EMPLOYMENT 87

between, and joint action by, a state and an airline company was evidently the central factor creating state action in a third case involving alleged sex discrimination in employment.[56]

## Tests of the Constitutionality of Discrimination

As the preceding cases make clear, the state action determination is subject to varying criteria in different courts. However, once state action has been found, equal protection analysis is not at an end. The next step is to apply the appropriate test of constitutionality. Discrimination based upon gender will be valid if a certain constitutional standard is satisfied. In determining whether discrimination is acceptable under the equal protection clause, the Supreme Court has developed three tests of differing stringency. The weak test requires only that the discrimination advance a legitimate government purpose and possess a reasonable basis in order to be constitutional. The intermediate test demands that the "discriminations must serve important governmental objectives and that the discriminatory means employed must be substantially related to the achievement of those objectives."[57] The strict test requires that the state demonstrate that the discrimination advances a compelling government interest and is no broader than necessary to achieve that interest.[58] The weak test is normally employed in constitutional assessment, but the strict test is used in the case of a "suspect" class—that is, a class that is "saddled with such disabilities, or subjected to such a history of purposeful unequal treatment, or relegated to such a position of political powerlessness as to command extraordinary protection from the majoritarian political process."[59] A plurality of the Supreme Court held in a case decided in 1973 that sex was a suspect criterion for classification,[60] but the view has never become a majority position. At the present time the intermediate test is used for sex discrimination.[61] (Indeed, its only clear use is for such discrimination.) However, while gender classifications are not subject to the most stringent test of constitutionality, discrimination against women has normally not survived judicial scrutiny.[62]

## CONCLUSIONS AND IMPLICATIONS REGARDING FERTILITY

The general picture that emerges is that ample authority exists for the federal government to suppress sex discrimination in employment. Legal protection for women can stem from the enactment of statutes by Congress or from the application of the Constitution by the judiciary. In the case of statutes Congress can ban sex discrimination by private parties, state and local governments, and agencies of the federal government by using its powers to regulate interstate commerce and to enforce the guarantee of equal protection. In the case of judicial application of the Constitution and its equal protection requirement, the courts can suppress sex discrimination in situations involving state action, though the line between state and private action is not always clear and may vary among different circuits of the federal judiciary.

If the rather impressive body of recent social science research is correct in maintaining that childbearing determines female employment rather than vice versa, the expansion of legal protections for women can be expected to promote fertility by increasing the likelihood that women can have children and still maintain jobs. If the expansion of legal protections does tend to foster childbearing, it is important to know how great an effect increased protection has in order to weigh its benefits against its burdens. In this context we must distinguish between effects on average family size and on population numbers. For three reasons, increased legal protections against sex discrimination can be expected not to have a large impact on average family size. First, many causes exist for any one behavioral pattern. Thus, law is just one of many factors that affect the course of fertility. Second, a particular cause of behavior rarely has a major impact; change in a cause is not often found to account for more than 10 percent of change in a behavior pattern such as fertility. Third, expanded legal protections for women will contribute to an already existing trend, not create one. The proportion of married women who are employed has been increasing steadily.[63] Since the factors that inhibit women from entering the labor force (including the presence of young children) have lost much of their effect,[64] the increasing proportion of wives who are employed seems primarily due to factors already operating that either push or draw women into employment. Inflation is currently pushing women into the job market and seems likely to continue.[65] Given the existence of a high rate of inflation, increased legal protection can enhance the drawing power of the job market for women in at least two ways. First, legal protection can reduce discrimination that restricts women's incomes.[66] Again, it will only promote an existing trend, for even now the income of working wives has an appreciable and growing impact on family income[67] and is being raised by federal government action attacking sex discrimination in employment.[68]

Increased legal protection can also make the job market more attractive for women by promoting child care facilities. At least one study indicates that child care facilities, in making it easier for women with children to work,[69] will foster childbearing.[70] If a recent decision of the U.S. Court of Appeals for the Ninth Circuit (which covers Arizona, California, Idaho, Montana, Nevada, Oregon, and Washington) is followed, denial of child care facilities can constitute sex discrimination.[71] Plaintiffs in the case were female students at public community colleges who alleged that, even though funds were available for the purpose, the colleges refused to provide child care facilities for the children of students and thereby made it difficult or impossible for women with children to acquire an education. The court, acknowledging that it was forced "to navigate somewhat at the margin of existing equal protection doctrine,"[72] held that a cause of action for sex discrimination existed under the equal protection clause if the plaintiffs could demonstrate that the policy of the colleges fell disproportionately on women and was intended, at least in part, to discriminate on the basis of sex. Discrimination could exist, according to the court, because child care facilities were important to the already existing educational effort. The court found that "the effect of the [Community College] District's child care policy is to render the entire 'package' of its educational programs of lesser worth to women than to men."[73] Consequently, when a government-produced effect falls overwhelmingly on females, the state need not have actually engaged in discriminatory conduct in order to run afoul of the equal protection clause; a failure to act will suffice if the failure results from a discriminatory intent. But here we are again dealing with an existing trend to which expanded legal protection for women can contribute; the need to provide child care facilities has already been the subject of judicial action and of congressional legislation.[74]

In short, the effect of increased legal protection for women on average family size is not likely to be dramatic. However, we must distinguish changes in average family size from the impact such changes might have on population numbers. While legal protection for employed women may increase average family size to only a small extent, it can be responsible for a substantial numerical increment to the population because of the large number of U.S. citizens presently in their childbearing years. If, because of increased legal protection in employment, a two-child average for women entering their childbearing period over the next two decades were to be increased by 5 percent (0.1 child), enhanced legal protection for women would generate 2 million additional people by the year 2000.[75] Population policymakers thus appear to be confronting a dilemma between civil rights and population control.

## NOTES

1. Commission on Population Growth and the American Future, *Population Growth and the American Future* 93 (Washington, D.C.: U.S. Gov't. Printing Office, 1972).
2. Richard Easterlin, *Factors in the Decline of Farm Family Fertility in the United States: Some Preliminary Research Results,* 63 Journal of American History 600, 609 (1976); Che-Fu Lee & M. Khan, *Factors Related to the Intention to Have Additional Children in the United States: A Reanalysis of Data from the 1965 and 1970 National Fertility Studies,* 15 Demography 337, 341 (1978). See Geraldine Terry, *Rival Explanations in the Work-Fertility Relationship,* 29 Population Studies 191, 203 (1975).
3. Linda Beckman, *Fertility Preferences and Social Exchange Theory,* 9 Journal of Applied Social Psychology 147, 165 (1979); Phyllis Ewer, E. Crimmins-Gardner, & R. Oliver, *An Analysis of the Relationship between Husband's Income, Family Size and Wife's Employment in the Early Stages of Marriage,* 41 Journal of Marriage & the Family 727 (1979); Michael Hout, *The Determinants of Marital Fertility in the United States, 1968–1970: Inferences from a Dynamic Model,* 15 Demography 139, 151 (1978); Lynn Smith-Lovin & Ann Tickamyer, *Nonrecursive Models of Labor Force Participation, Fertility Behavior, and Sex Role Attitudes,* 43 American Sociological Review 541, 554 (1978); Terry, *supra* note 2, at 199; Helen Ware, *Fertility and Work-Force*

*Participation: The Experience of Melbourne Wives,* 30 Population Studies 413, 427 (1976). *See* Pamela Cain, "The Determinants of Marital Labor Supply, Fertility and Sex-Role Attitudes" (paper presented at the 1979 meeting of the Population Association of America, April 25-28, 1979); James McCabe & M. Rosenzweig, *Female Employment Creation and Family Size,* in Population and Development 322, 335, 347 (Ronald G. Ridker, ed.; Baltimore: Johns Hopkins University Press, 1976); James Sweet, "The Impact of Recent Fertility and Nuptiality Trends in the Employment and Work Experience of Young Women" (Working Paper 79-17, Center for Demography & Ecology, University of Wisconsin-Madison, 1979). *Contra* James Cramer, *Fertility and Female Employment: Problems of Causal Direction,* 45 American Sociological Review 167 (1980).

4. Smith-Lovin & Tickamyer, *supra* note 3, at 554.

5. A national survey conducted in the early 1970s found definite differences between the sexes in the goals sought in and through jobs. Men placed a higher value than women on the intrinsic aspects of work; that is, men were more concerned with whether a job was interesting, allowed workers to develop their abilities, and permitted them to see the results of their efforts. Women placed greater emphasis on whether a job provided convenient travel to and from the workplace, good hours and pleasant physical surroundings, and freedom from conflicting demands. Compared to men, women seemed to have less of an attachment to work and to want "as little interference with their nonwork roles as possible." Arne L. Kalleberg, "Work Values, Job Rewards and Job Satisfaction: A Theory of the Quality of Work Experience" 65 (unpublished Ph.D. dissertation, University of Wisconsin-Madison, August, 1975).

Only about one in nine American women between the ages of eighteen and twenty-four in 1979 expected to have no children during her lifetime, and only another one in nine expected to have just one child; fully three out of four expected to have two or more children. Bureau of the Census, U.S. Department of Commerce, *Fertility of American Women: June 1979,* Current Population Reports, Series P-20, No. 358, at 20 (1980). These statistics suggest that women generally define childbearing as a central aspect of their lives that takes priority over employment.

6. Rodolfo Bulatao & Fred Arnold, *Relationships between the Value and Cost of Children and Fertility: Cross-Cultural Evidence,* in 1 International Population Conference, Mexico, 1977 141, 146, 155 (International Union for the Scientific Study of Population, 1977); Rodolfo Bulatao, *Values and Disvalues of Children in Successive Childbearing Decisions,* 18 Demography 1 (1981); "Attitudes about Children: Report to Respondents" (Survey Research Center, Institute for Social Research, University of Michigan, October, 1976). *See* Christine Bachrach, D. Dawson, & J. Ridley, "The Effects of the Depression on Fertility and Fertility Control: The Experience of the 1901-1910 Birth Cohorts" (paper presented at 1979 meeting of the Population Association of America, April 25-28, 1979). *See also* Arland Thornton, *Fertility and Income, Consumption Aspirations, and Child Quality Standards,* 16 Demography 157 (1979).

7. Frank Mott, *The National Longitudinal Survey of Mature Women's Cohort: A Socioeconomic Overview,* in Women's Changing Roles at Home and on the Job 23, 52, 54 (Special Report No. 26 of the National Commission for Manpower Policy, Washington, D.C.: U.S. Gov't. Printing Office, 1978); Carl Rosenfeld & V. Perrella, *Why Women Start and Stop Working: A Study in Mobility,* 88 Monthly Labor Review 1077 (1965); Henry Gordon & Kenneth Kammeyer, *The Gainful Employment of Women with Small Children,* 42 Journal of Marriage & the Family 327 (1980).

8. Edward Hudson & D. Jorgenson, *Energy Prices and the U.S. Economy, 1972-1976,* 18 Natural Resources Journal 877 (1978).

Resource shortages and concomitant increases in the cost of resources are one manifestation of population pressures. Lester Brown, The Twenty-Ninth Day 161-91 (New York: Norton, 1978).

9. Between 1970 and 1973, per capita income in constant dollars — that is, per capita income adjusted for inflation in order to show changes in purchasing power — increased steadily, rising a total of about 12 percent. The shortages of domestic sources of oil made apparent by the Arab oil embargo of 1973 and subsequent oil price rises interrupted the trend toward greater purchasing power per person, and it was not until 1977 that per capita income in constant dollars exceeded the 1973 level. Bureau of the Census, U.S. Department of Commerce, *Money Income in 1978 of Households in the United States,* Current Population Reports, Series P-60, No. 121, at 2 (1980).

10. It must be kept in mind that, while women now say they expect to have an average of two children each when they answer simple, straightforward questions, more sophisticated research suggests that women have a strong underlying preference for larger families — a preference that would presumably be fulfilled if conditions permitted. *Compare* Bureau of the Census, U.S. Department of Commerce, *supra* note 5, at 9, *with* Judith Blake, *Can We Believe Recent Data on Birth Expectations in the United States?* 11 Demography 25 (1974) *and with* Lolagene Coombs, *Underlying Family-Size Preferences and Reproductive Behavior,* 10 Studies in Family Planning 25, 29-30 (1979). *See also* Lolagene Coombs, *Reproductive Goals and Achieved Fertility: A Fifteen-Year Perspective,* 16 Demography 523 (1979).

11. The demographer explained:

> It is often assumed that the present-day "women's liberation" movement is essentially anti-natalist in ideology and that its effects will be anti-natalist as well. Actually, however, the main thrust of the movement's stand is supportive of motherhood for all; what is decried is the relative disadvantage that women experience because of childbearing and rearing. In effect, women's liberation is concerned with lowering the exclusionary barriers for women in the labor force, opening up educational channels, elevating women's awareness of subtle forms of discrimination against them in the outside world, and supporting women's right to have families as well. Rather than concerning itself with the atypical spinster or childless woman, the movement has gained

popularity through its recognition of the problems of women who have already made a choice to be mothers and who then are dissatisfied with their impaired occupational chances, or who find motherhood less than they expected it to be and wish to switch gears.... However, although the movement has pitched its appeal to women who have already made their reproductive choices and urged them to seek out an alternative identity as well, its general philosophy for all women is one of combining marriage and motherhood, on the one hand, with a nonfamilial role, on the other. Indeed, it is this militant statement that women should not have to make a choice that gives the movement wide appeal.

Judith Blake, *Coercive Pronatalism and American Population Policy,* in Aspects of Population Growth Policy 81, 93 (Vol. VI of the Research Reports of the U.S. Commission on Population Growth and the American Future, Robert Parke, Jr. & Charles F. Westoff, eds.; Washington, D.C.: U.S. Gov't. Printing Office, 1972).

12. "The Congress shall have power ... to regulate commerce ... among the several States ..." U.S. Constitution, art. I, § 8, cl. 3.

13. 42 U.S.C. § 2000e *et seq.* (1976); 29 U.S.C. § 206(d) (1976).

14. *See* Nat'l League of Cities v Usery, 426 U.S. 833 (1976); Heart of Atlanta Motel, Inc. v United States, 379 U.S. 241 (1964); Katzenbach v McClung, 379 U.S. 294 (1964); United States v Darby, 312 U.S. 100 (1941).

15. Fry v United States, 421 U.S. 542, 547 (1975).

16. Nat'l League of Cities v Usery, *supra* note 14.

17. U.S. Constitution, amend. XIV, §§ 1, 5.

18. Equal Employment Opportunity Act of 1972, 42 U.S.C. § 2000e *et seq.* (1976); United States v Virginia, 620 F.2d 1018 (4th Cir. 1979), *cert. denied,* 101 S.Ct. 589 (1980); Shawer v Indiana Univ., 602 F.2d 1161 (3rd Cir. 1979); Blake v City of Los Angeles, 595 F.2d 1367 (9th Cir. 1979), *cert. denied,* 446 U.S. 928 (1980); United States v New Hampshire, 539 F.2d 277 (1st Cir. 1976), *cert. denied,* 429 U.S. 1023 (1976).

Equal Pay Act, 29 U.S.C. § 206(d) (1976): Marshall v A & M Consolidated Ind. School Dist., 605 F.2d 186 (5th Cir. 1979).

19. The due process clause of the Fifth Amendment applies an equal protection requirement to the federal government. Hampton v Wong, 426 U.S. 88 (1976). However, Congress is not given express authority to enact legislation in support of the requirement.

20. U.S. Constitution, art. I, § 8, cl. 1 and 18. *See generally* United States v Butler, 297 U.S. 1 (1936).

21. 29 U.S.C. § 206(d) (1976).

22. Laurence H. Tribe, American Constitutional Law 992-93 (Mineola, N.Y.: Foundation Press, 1978).

23. The equal protection clause of the Fourteenth Amendment applies to states, and the due process clause of the Fifth Amendment applies the same requirement to the federal government. However, there may be significant

national interests that justify action by the federal government in spite of the equal protection guarantee but that do not exist for action by a state government. Hampton v Wong, 426 U.S. 88, 100 (1976).

24. Burton v Wilmington Parking Auth., 365 U.S. 715 (1961); Civil Rights Cases, 109 U.S. 3 (1883).

25. Flagg Bros., Inc. v Brooks, 436 U.S. 149 (1978); Jackson v Metropolitan Edison Co., 419 U.S. 345 (1974).

26. Slaughter House Cases, 83 U.S. (16 Wall) 36, 71 (1873); Washington v Davis, 426 U.S. 229, 239 (1976).

27. *E.g.,* Grafton v Brooklyn Law School, 478 F.2d 1137, 1142 (2d Cir. 1973); Granfield v Catholic Univ., 530 F.2d 1035, 1046 n.29 (D.C. Cir. 1976), *cert. denied,* 429 U.S. 821 (1976); Greco v Orange Memorial Hospital Corp., 513 F.2d 873, 879 (5th Cir. 1975), *cert. denied,* 423 U.S. 1000 (1975). Note, *State Action: Theories for Applying Constitutional Restrictions to Private Activity,* 74 Columbia Law Review 656, 657-58 (1974).

28. Cases to date have involved the equal protection guarantee of the Fourteenth Amendment rather than the Fifth Amendment. See note 23 *supra.*

29. In addition to cases involving employment, cases will be examined in which sex discrimination allegedly occurred in admissions to institutions of higher education. Educational attainment appears to have no direct causal impact on fertility, but it does directly affect income, though perhaps not as much among females as among males. Females are less likely than males to obtain a college education, evidently due partly to sex discrimination, and to the extent that elimination of sex discrimination in the educational system increases the income of women, economic constraints on childbearing are reduced. Ronald Rindfuss, L. Bumpass, & C. St. John, *Education and Fertility: Implications for the Roles Women Occupy,* 45 American Sociological Review 431 (1980); Kenneth Wilson, *Toward an Improved Explanation of Income Attainment: Recalibrating Education and Occupation,* 84 American Journal of Sociology 684 (1978); William Sewell, A. Haller, & G. Ohlendorf, *The Educational and Early Occupational Status Attainment Process: Replication and Revision,* 35 American Sociological Review 1014, 1023, 1025 (1970); William Sewell, *Inequality of Opportunity for Higher Education,* 36 American Sociological Review 793, 796, 804 (1971); Karl Alexander & B. Eckland, *Sex Differences in the Educational Attainment Process,* 39 American Sociological Review 668 (1974).

30. Weise v Syracuse Univ., 522 F.2d 397 (2d Cir. 1975).

31. 42 U.S.C. § 1983 (1976) reads in full:

> Every person who, under color of any statute, ordinance, regulation, custom, or usage, of any State or Territory, subjects, or causes to be subjected, any citizen of the United States or other person within the jurisdiction thereof to the deprivation of any rights, privileges, or immunities secured by the Constitution and laws, shall be liable to the party injured in an action at law, suit in equity, or other proper proceeding for redress.

32. Flagg Bros, Inc. v Brooks, *supra* note 25, at 157. Faced with an alleged

LEGAL PROTECTION AND FEMALE EMPLOYMENT 95

violation of the due process clause of the Fourteenth Amendment in a suit filed under 42 U.S.C. § 1983, the Supreme Court, in discussing the "under color of any statute" requirement, stated:

> [O]nly a State or a private person whose action "may fairly be treated as that of the State itself" may deprive [an individual] of "an interest encompassed within the Fourteenth Amendment's protection." Thus, the only issue presented by this case is whether [defendant's] action may fairly be attributed to the State of New York.

The language of this statement suggests that the Supreme Court does not distinguish the state action requirement of the Fourteenth Amendment and the "under color of statute" requirement of § 1983 but, rather, treats them as identical prerequisites in claims of constitutional violation. The "under color of ordinance or regulation" requirement of § 1983 will probably be considered the equivalent of state action too. On the other hand, state action under the Fourteenth Amendment may not be as broad as the "custom or usage" of a state under § 1983. However, the "custom or usage" criterion is not an issue in any of the cases discussed in this chapter, and it therefore need not be considered further.

33. Throughout the opinion, the court discusses "state action" and the "state action standard." Weise v Syracuse Univ., 522 F.2d at 403-8.
34. *Id.* at 406.
35. Stewart v New York Univ., 430 F. Supp. 1305 (S.D. N.Y. 1976).
36. *Id.* at 1311 n.6, 1311-12.
37. Ludtke v Kuhn, 461 F. Supp. 86 (S.D. N.Y. 1978).
38. *Id.* at 96. The relevant facts and law on the state action issue appear on pages 92-96.
39. *Id.* at 92.
40. *Id.* at 95-96.
41. Braden v Univ. of Pittsburgh, 552 F.2d 948 (3d Cir. 1977); Rackin v Univ. of Pennsylvania, 386 F. Supp. 992 (E.D. Pa. 1974).
42. 552 F.2d at 960-61; 386 F. Supp. at 996-99.

In the latter case, where state funds constituted only one-tenth of the operating budget, the court emphasized that the funds represented one-fourth of the "hard-core" budget — that is, the budget that directly affected the operating deficit of the institution and largely determined the degree to which the institution achieved its primary goals of education and research. 386 F. Supp. at 997.

43. 522 F.2d at 960.
44. 386 F. Supp. at 1005. The same point is made on page 997.
45. 552 F.2d at 959; 386 F. Supp. at 997, 1001, 1004.
46. Cannon v Univ. of Chicago, 559 F.2d 1063 (7th Cir. 1977), *rev'd. on statutory grounds,* 441 U.S. 677 (1979); Cohen v Illinois Inst. of Technology, 524 F.2d 818 (7th Cir. 1975), *cert. denied,* 425 U.S. 943 (1976).
47. Cannon v Univ. of Chicago, *supra* note 46, at 1069, 1070.

48. Braden v Univ. of Pittsburgh, 552 F.2d 948, 964–65 (3d Cir. 1977).
49. Lamb v Rantoul, 561 F.2d 409 (1st Cir. 1977), *aff'g* Melanson v Rantoul, 421 F. Supp. 492 (D. R.I. 1976).

The school offers the bachelor's and master's degrees in architecture, design, and fine arts. 65 Bulletin of Rhode Island School of Design, 1978–1979 (September, 1978).

50. 561 F.2d at 411.
51. R.I. Gen. Laws §§ 16–35–1 to 16–35–4, 16–37–3 to 16–37–5 (1956).
52. *Id.* at §§ 16–46–1, 16–46–2.
53. Brown v Frito-Lay, Inc., 15 FEP Cases 1055 (D. Kan. 1976).
54. Nat'l Organization of Women v Bank of California, 5 EPD ¶ 8510 (N.D. Cal. 1973).
55. Cal. Financial Code §§ 99–3580 (1968) (West); Cal. Gov't Code §§ 16506, 16670 (1963) (West); Cal. Gov't Code § 45308.1 (Supp. 1980) (West).

The defendant bank was incorporated in California and chartered under the National Bank Act. I Moody's Bank and Finance Manual 733 (New York: Moody's Investors Service, 1979). As such, the state had the statutory authority to regulate it. Cal. Financial Code § 100 (1968) (West).

56. Masco v United Airlines, 13 EPD ¶ 11,578 (W.D. Pa. 1976).
57. Wengler v Druggists Mutual Ins. Co., 446 U.S. 142, 150 (1980).
58. Dandridge v Williams, 397 U.S. 471, 485 (1969); Dunn v Blumstein, 405 U.S. 330, 342–43 (1972); Note, *Of Interests, Fundamental and Compelling: The Emerging Constitutional Balance*, 57 Boston University Law Rev. 462 (1977).
59. San Antonio Ind. School Dist. v Rodriguez, 411 U.S. 1, 28 (1973).

The strict test is also employed when state action seriously infringes on a fundamental constitutional right. Zablocki v Redhail, 434 U.S. 374 (1978).

60. Frontiero v Richardson, 411 U.S. 677 (1973).
61. Wengler v Druggists Mutual Ins. Co., *supra* note 57. *Accord*, Tribe, *supra* note 22, at 1082–92.
62. Wengler v Druggists Mutual Ins. Co., *supra* note 57; Orr v Orr, 440 U.S. 268 (1979); Califano v Goldfarb, 430 U.S. 199 (1977); Weinberger v Weisenfeld, 420 U.S. 636 (1975); Stanton v Stanton, 421 U.S. 7 (1975); Frontiero v Richardson, *supra* note 60; Reed v Reed, 404 U.S. 71 (1971).
63. The proportion of married women living with their husbands and in the labor force was 24 percent in 1950, 31 percent in 1960, 41 percent in 1970, and 48 percent in 1978. Bureau of the Census, U.S. Department of Commerce, Statistical Abstract of the United States: 1979, 100th ed., 401 (Washington, D.C.: U.S. Gov't. Printing Office, 1979).
64. Linda Waite, *Working Wives: 1940–1960*, 41 American Sociological Review 65 (1976); Jean Darian, *Factors Influencing the Rising Labor Force Participation Rates of Married Women with Pre-School Children*, 56 Social Science Quarterly 614 (1976).

The proportion of married women, living with their husbands, who had children under six years of age and who were in the labor force was 12 percent in 1950, 19 percent in 1960, 30 percent in 1970, and 42 percent in 1978. Bureau of the Census, *supra* note 63, at 401. An examination of the ratios of these proportions to those in note 63 *supra* shows that the labor force participation rate among wives with young children grew increasingly similar to the rate among all wives between 1950 and 1978. Thus, the labor force participation rate of all wives was twice that of wives with young children in 1950, but only slightly larger in 1978.

65. Since 1973, consumer prices have increased by no less than 5.8 percent annually. The average annual increase was 1.3 percent in the 1960-1965 period and 4.2 percent in the 1965-1970 period. Bureau of the Census, U.S. Department of Commerce, Statistical Abstract of the United States: 1980, 101st ed., 478 (Washington, D.C.: U.S. Gov't. Printing Office, 1980).

The inflation experienced by the United States since 1973 is attributable in large part to shortages of resources. L. Brown, *supra* note 8. Given the rapid increase in world population, shortages can be expected to get worse. World population numbers are rising each year by some 80 million — an annual increment that is substantially larger than it was ten years ago. Bureau of the Census, U.S. Department of Commerce, World Population 1977 18 (Washington, D.C.: U.S. Gov't. Printing Office, 1978).

66. *See* Patricia Taylor, *Income Inequality in the Federal Civilian Government,* 44 American Sociological Review 468, 475-78 (1979).

In comparing the earnings of husbands and wives, a study of data from a 1967 national survey concluded:

> Wives earn about half as much as their husbands. Less than half of this difference can be attributed to the fact that wives work less and have worked only part of their adult lives. The remaining difference in the income of husbands and wives is no doubt due to a combination of direct discrimination against women in the labor market, institutional arrangements that constrain the opportunities of married women, and norms that permit (or require) married women to consider the non-income attributes of jobs.

Donald Treiman & K. Terrell, *Sex and the Process of Status Attainment: A Comparison of Working Women and Men,* 40 American Sociological Review 174, 198 (1975). Other research supports the conclusion that sex discrimination seriously affects the earnings of women. A study of married men and women in the period between 1962 and 1973 found that married "[w]omen have not experienced equality of economic opportunity, and the 1973 data indicate only a minute diminution of this inequality"; that the inequality was not attributable to sex differences in education, occupation, or family background; and that sex differences in work experience and time in the labor force accounted for only about one-fifth of the inequality, leaving four-fifths due to other factors, such as discrimination. David Featherman & R. Hauser, *Sexual Inequalities and Socioeconomic Achievement in the U.S., 1962-1973,* 41 American Sociological Review 462, 480 (1976). *See* U.S. Commission on Civil Rights, Social Indicators of Equality for Minorities and Women 65 (Washington, D.C.: U.S. Gov't. Printing

Office, 1978). *See generally* P. Hudis, *Commitment to Work and to Family: Marital Status Differences in Women's Earnings,* 38 Journal of Marriage & the Family 267 (1976); Wendy Wolf & R. Rosenfeld, *Sex Structure of Occupations and Job Mobility,* 56 Social Forces 823 (1978).

67. Valerie Oppenheimer, *The Sociology of Women's Economic Role in the Family,* 42 American Sociological Review 387, 400 (1977); Mott, *supra* note 7, at 47.

68. Andrea Beller, *Title VII and the Male/Female Earnings Gap: An Econometric Analysis,* 1 Harvard Women's Law Journal 157 (1978). *See generally* Paul Burstein, *Equal Employment Opportunity Legislation and the Income of Women and Nonwhites,* 44 American Sociological Review 367 (1979).

69. Linda Beckman, *The Relative Rewards and Costs of Parenthood and Employment for Employed Women,* 2 Psychology of Women Quarterly 215, 231-32 (1978); Darian, *supra* note 64, at 621; Michael Landsberger, *Children's Age as a Factor Affecting the Simultaneous Determination of Consumption and Labor Supply,* 40 Southern Economic Journal 279, 288 (1973).

70. Josefina Card, *The Malleability of Fertility-Related Attitudes and Behavior in a Filipino Migrant Sample,* 15 Demography 459, 475 (1978). *Contra,* Mary G. Powers & Joseph Salvo, "Fertility and Child Care Arrangements as Mechanisms of Status Articulation" (paper presented at 1980 meeting of the American Sociological Association, August 27-31, 1980).

71. De La Cruz v Tormey, 582 F.2d 45 (9th Cir. 1978), *cert. denied,* 441 U.S. 965 (1979).

72. *Id.* at 50-51.

73. *Id.* at 56.

74. *E.g.,* I.R.C. §§ 44A, 188. See S. Rep. No. 92-437, 92d Cong., 1st Sess. (1971), reprinted in [1971] U.S. Code Congressional & Administrative News 1918, 1971.

75. Calculated from the Series II projection in Bureau of the Census, U.S. Department of Commerce, *Projections of the Population of the United States: 1977 to 2050,* Current Population Reports, Series P-25, No. 704, at 6 (1977).

# 6 HOUSING POLICIES PROHIBITING CHILDREN

Another factor that can have an impact on childbearing (even though its impact is not the primary goal of proponents) is policies that exclude children from housing being rented or sold. As such policies become prevalent, childless couples who want to become parents but need new housing to do so will find it difficult to locate adequate quarters. A housing market in which people find it difficult to move, combined with inadequate space in currently occupied housing, has been found to curtail childbearing.[1]

A 1980 nationwide study of rental housing has provided the first good picture of the incidence of child-exclusion policies.[2] The study reported that one out of four rental units excludes children. The principal reasons for the exclusion were higher maintenance costs and the problem posed by unsupervised and noisy children. However, housing and neighborhood quality did not differ between units that excluded children and units that accepted them. Instances of child-exclusion policies were thus not infrequent, and some evidence indicated that they had become more prevalent during the 1970s. Indeed, several states have enacted legislation forbidding such policies.[3]

Child-exclusion policies can reduce the birth rate by encouraging childlessness, and voluntary childlessness is important in curtailing population growth because relatively few couples who become parents have just one child. If a couple decide to become parents, they will almost certainly have at least two children.[4] Child-exclusion policies can promote childlessness both by increasing the burden involved in having children and by permitting people who want to remain childless to live near, and receive support from, other adults who have the same commitment.[5] The policies are not, of course, the only factor leading individuals to choose childlessness; the child-free lifestyle possesses other attractions unrelated to housing prospects.[6] However, the acceptance of voluntary childlessness is increasing,[7] and child-exclusion policies can be expected to affect its incidence since one-third of all occupied housing space in the United States is composed of rental units.[8]

The legal aspects of child-exclusion policies involve two separate constitutional questions. The first, and most quickly answered, is whether statutes forbidding the policies are valid. There appears to have been no court case to date challenging the constitutionality of such statutes, but if one were to be brought, the statutes would probably be upheld on the ground that they protect family life.[9] The second constitutional question is whether child-exclusion policies are valid when no statute exists to forbid them. This is the more important question, since few states have statutes forbidding the policies.[10]

Two constitutional guarantees are presently applicable to child-exclusion policies: due process and equal protection.[11] However, the guarantees are restrictions only on state action; they do not protect an individual against the conduct of another who is acting solely as a private party.[12] Accordingly, we must determine whether state action can be found in the conduct of a private individual who refuses to rent or sell housing to people with children.

## STATE ACTION

In considering the conditions under which state action exists, we must examine the nature of the relationship between government and the development and operation of housing. State action has not been found in cases involving private landlords whose buildings were constructed with mortgage money insured by the federal government.[13] Neither has it been found in cases where a landlord's buildings were the beneficiaries of financial subsidies from the federal government, partial exemptions from state real property taxes, or reduced utility rates.[14] However, financial benefits from government to private landlords, combined with substantial regulations imposed by government, have been sufficient to generate a finding of state action,[15] especially when the housing was built on land obtained by an urban renewal agency with the power of eminent domain.[16] Accordingly, state action can inhere in housing from which children are excluded.

State action can also result from the conduct of the person who is selling or renting housing if a governmental entity is sufficiently involved with that conduct. A judicial order of eviction secured by a landlord has been held by a number of courts to be insufficient by itself to warrant a finding of state action,[17] but there is precedent strongly supporting the contrary position. The Supreme Court has determined the constitutionality of, and hence found state action in, a state statute prescribing the conditions and procedures for obtaining a court order to evict a tenant.[18] The Court has also held that judicial enforcement of real property covenants results in state action.[19] These findings reflect a more general principle: While the mere existence of a statute authorizing a procedure to be undertaken by private parties without the involvement of the judicial system is not an adequate basis for state action, state action will occur when the judiciary orders private parties to act and a person is deprived of property to which he or she has a claim.[20] Court-ordered eviction appears to be sufficient to satisfy the criterion for state action prescribed by the Supreme Court.

When faced with child-exclusion policies, then, courts may find state action in the development and operation of the housing involved or in the use of the judicial system to evict tenants. We now turn to an examination of the constitutional dimension of those policies.

## DUE PROCESS AND EQUAL PROTECTION

Three constitutional questions exist regarding child-exclusion policies in housing:

1. Are the policies invalid because they interfere with the constitutionally protected right of childbearing?

2. Are the policies invalid because they interfere with the right of a family to live together?
3. Are the policies invalid because they create classifications that distinguish persons who have children from persons who do not?

The first two questions arise from the guarantee of due process; the third stems from the guarantee of equal protection. The due process clauses of the Fifth and Fourteenth Amendments contain an express protection of "liberty" that has been held to constitute an umbrella guarding decisions to have (or not to have) a child[21] and to live together as a family.[22] The equal protection clause of the Fourteenth Amendment limits the ability of government to establish classifications.[23] State action that seriously interferes with a person's decisions regarding procreation or family living arrangements, or that creates a suspect class, is valid only if it advances a compelling governmental interest by the narrowest possible means.[24] If there is no serious infringement of rights or no suspect class, the government will prevail as long as a reasonable basis exists for its action.[25]

The most recent case dealing with child-exclusion policies was decided by the Florida Supreme Court. A condominium complex prohibited the sale of a unit to anyone with children under twelve years of age, but a unit was sold to an individual with a young child. The court concluded that the exclusion policy was facially valid.[26] In reaching its decision, the court employed the reasonable basis test on the ground that the policy created a classification by age that did not seriously affect a fundamental constitutional right or create a suspect class.[27] The court found a reasonable basis in the different housing needs and desires of different age groups:

> The urbanization of this country, requiring substantial portions of our population to live closer together, coupled with the desire for varying types of family units and recreational activities have brought about new concepts in living accommodations. There are residential units designed specifically for young adults, for families with young children, and for senior citizens. The desires and demands of each category are different.[28]

The court failed to explain why the policy in question was not a serious intrusion into the constitutionally protected decision about childbearing, as the lower appellate court had found. However, the

# HOUSING POLICIES PROHIBITING CHILDREN 103

view that no such intrusion existed can be justified under U.S. Supreme Court precedents. For instance, the action of a state in providing indigent women funds for childbirth services but not for abortions has been held not to be a direct and substantial infringement on decisions regarding procreation.[29] Also, a state regulation imposing a maximum on welfare assistance for recipients of Aid to Families with Dependent Children, even though the maximum grant was less than the state-calculated needs of large families, has been held not to be a serious infringement on childbearing decisions.[30] If decisions regarding procreation are not seriously affected by an individual's inability to obtain financial aid for an abortion or for supporting children, the inability to obtain certain housing because of children should also constitute no serious infringement on childbearing decisions. Lack of access to necessary or desired finances and lack of access to necessary or desired housing are equally distant from the constitutionally protected activity of procreation. Accordingly, insofar as the right of childbearing is concerned, the reasonable basis test is the appropriate standard.

One U.S. Court of Appeals has utilized a similar line of reasoning in a case involving a state university that barred children from the housing it made available to married students.[31] In response to a challenge on the ground that the distinction between married students with and without children created a classification denying equal protection, the court rejected the use of the compelling interest test. It cited three reasons for its decision: There is no constitutionally guaranteed right to housing of a particular type or quality; housing for students falls within an area traditionally committed to the discretion of school authorities; and the child-exclusion policy in dispute did not directly and substantially interfere with childbearing. Thus, the court concluded:

> The University here is not interfering with the marital privacy of the plaintiffs or their unquestioned natural right to bring up their children. They are totally free to procreate and educate their offspring—the only question is whether the University is constitutionally mandated to provide them campus housing to perform their protected prerogatives.[32]

Finding dangers to children from fire, construction, and traffic on campus, the court upheld the policy.

The application of the reasonable basis test to child-exclusion policies receives support from cases that have challenged the establishment of community subdivisions devoted to the elderly. In response to the challenges, the reasonable basis test has been used and the government action creating the communities has been upheld.[33] These decisions are in line with the Supreme Court, which has concluded that old age is not a suspect class under the guarantee of equal protection and thus that the less stringent test is the appropriate standard for the class:

> While the treatment of the aged in this nation has not been wholly free of discrimination, such persons, unlike, say, those who have been discriminated against on the basis of race or national origin, have not experienced a history of purposeful unequal treatment or been subjected to unique disabilities on the basis of stereotyped characteristics not truly indicative of their abilities.[34]

The Court's reasoning can be applied equally well to people with children, since our society provides distinct benefits for them.[35] Indeed, the Supreme Court has already stated, though arguably in dictum, that family size is not a suspect criterion for a classification.[36] Accordingly, the reasonable basis test can be used for the classification between parents and nonparents created by child-exclusion policies in housing. Under the reasonable basis test the policies can easily be upheld.[37]

Even if child-exclusion policies can be upheld under the standard of reasonableness on the ground that they do not seriously affect the constitutionally protected childbearing decision or establish a suspect class, we must still ask whether the policies are invalid because they interfere with the ability of a family to live together. The decision of the Supreme Court in *Moore v City of East Cleveland* has a potential bearing on the question.[38] In *Moore* a city ordinance limited occupancy of a dwelling unit to members of a single family, but the term *family* was defined in such a manner as to exclude the appellant grandmother and her two grandsons, who were first cousins. The appellant, who was fined twenty-five dollars and sentenced to five days in jail for violating the ordinance, challenged the legislation as violative of the liberty protected by the guarantee of due process. The Supreme Court overturned the conviction on the grounds that the ordinance was unconstitutional. A four-member plurality agreed with the appellant that the ordinance deprived her of freedom of choice in the realm of family life. They concluded that constitutional protection must be given to the extended family as well as to the nuclear family of husband, wife, and children.[39]

The plurality decision appears to have placed the family interest in residing together under the protection of the compelling interest test.[40] The ordinance was found invalid under the test because the means used by the city were not sufficiently narrow to promote only the governmental objectives claimed to be at stake—namely, the prevention of overcrowded housing, the alleviation of traffic congestion, and the elimination of unnecessary financial burdens on the school system. These goals were not attainable under the ordinance because, for example, any number of unmarried children could live with their parents.

Similar reasoning was employed by a lower state court several years prior to *Moore*. A municipal ordinance required that at least 70 percent of all units in an apartment complex have no more than one bedroom, that a maximum of 25 percent of the units have two bedrooms, and that no more than 5 percent have three bedrooms. The admitted purpose of the ordinance was to minimize the number of children in the municipality in order to limit expenditures for schools and, hence, taxes. The court held that the ordinance violated the equal protection clause because there is a constitutional "right to live as a family, and not be subject to a limitation on the number of members of that family in order to reside any place."[41]

Does the right of a family to live together invalidate child-exclusion policies? The two cases we have discussed involved ordinances with citywide application, and it was probably this feature that created the constitutional violation. The ordinances were not limited to specific geographic areas within the municipalities and were therefore responsible for serious infringements on the right of a family to live together. It is doubtful whether the compelling interest test will or should be used for child-exclusion policies enforced in the sale and rental of housing pursuant to ordinances having only limited geographic application. For example, in a decision rendered by a lower state court prior to *Moore*, the developer of a large tract of land for mobile homes reserved a portion of the tract for persons who were at least twenty-one years of age.[42] Finding state action in the judicial enforcement of the restriction, the court held that the policy was constitutional because it reasonably advanced the legitimate purpose of reducing noise and other disturbances in a residential area. The court noted, however, that there was no evidence of a housing shortage in the area for families with children — a suggestion that child-exclusion policies would meet a different judicial fate if they were enforced throughout a large geographic area and created a housing shortage.

In summary, child-exclusion policies, when they do not stem from legislation having wide geographic application, do not seriously interfere with constitutionally protected decisions to have children or live together as a family. Neither do child-exclusion policies create a suspect classification. Accordingly, state action promoting the policies will be constitutionally evaluated according to whether it possesses a reasonable basis, which may easily be found in the elimination of the noise and damage caused by children. Moreover, in the absence of any legislation requiring child-exclusion policies, the decisions of private individuals not to sell or rent housing to people with children will normally not involve state action. Child-exclusion policies thus have the potential to become more prevalent and thus to provide a significant stimulus to childlessness.

## NOTES

1. Marcus Felson & M. Solaun, *The Fertility-Inhibiting Effect of Crowded Apartment Living in a Tight Housing Market,* 80 American Journal of Sociology 1410 (1975); James P. Curry & Gayle Scriven, *The Relationship between Apartment Living and Fertility for Blacks, Mexican-Americans, and Other Americans in Racine, Wisconsin,* 15 Demography 477 (1978).

2. Mary Ellen Colten & Robert Marans, *Restrictive Rental Practices and Their Impact on Families,* 1 Population Research and Policy Review 43 (1982).

3. Five states expressly prohibit child-exclusion policies, but some of the statutes include exceptions — for example, for subdivisions devoted entirely to adults. The five states are Arizona, Delaware, Massachusetts, New Jersey, and New York. Ariz. Rev. Stat. Ann. §§ 33-303, 33-1317 (Supp. 1980-81); Del. Code Ann. tit. 25 § 6503 (1974); Mass. Gen. Laws Ann. ch. 151B, § 4(11) (West Supp. 1981); N.J. Stat. Ann. § 2A:170-92 (West 1971); N.Y. Real Prop. Law §§ 236, 237 (McKinney 1968) (Supp. 1980-81).

4. Bureau of the Census, U.S. Department of Commerce, *Fertility of American Women: June 1979,* Current Population Reports, Series P-20, No. 358, at 20, 28 (1980).

5. For research on the importance of group support in the decision to remain childless, see Sharon Houseknecht, *Reference Group Support for Voluntary Childlessness: Evidence for Conformity*, 39 Journal of Marriage & the Family 285 (1977); Sharon Houseknecht, *Timing of the Decision to Remain Voluntarily Childless: Evidence for Continuous Socialization,* 4 Psychology of Women Quarterly 81 (1979).

6. Larry D. Barnett & Richard MacDonald, *A Study of the Membership of the National Organization for Non-Parents,* 23 Social Biology 297, 303-5 (1976); Jean E. Veevers, Childless by Choice 49-59 (Toronto: Butterworth, 1980).

7. Dudley Poston, Jr. & Erin Gotard, *Trends in Childlessness in the United States, 1910-1975,* 24 Social Biology 212 (1977). Elizabeth Douvan, "The Marriage Role: 1957-1976" (Survey Research Center, University of Michigan, 1978). *See also* Judith Blake, *Is Zero Preferred? American Attitudes Toward Childnessness in the 1970s,* 41 Journal of Marriage & the Family 245 (1979).

Among American women 18 to 24 years old in 1979, 11.4 percent expected to have no children. Bureau of the Census, U.S. Department of Commerce, *Fertility of American Women: June 1979,* Current Population Reports, Series P-20, No. 358, at 20 (1980).

8. Bureau of the Census, U.S. Department of Commerce, Statistical Abstract of the United States: 1980, 101st ed., 793 (Washington, D.C.: U.S. Gov't. Printing Office, 1980).

The impact of child-exclusion policies will undoubtedly be greatest in rental housing. Owners of single-family homes will not often have any reason for such a policy, and few homeowners are found in multiple-family buildings such as condominiums. *Id.* at 795.

9. See Village of Belle Terre v Boraas, 416 U.S. 1 (1974).

10. *See* note 3 *supra.* Moreover, one state (Illinois) recently repealed its statute. Ill. Ann. Stat. ch. 80, § 37 (Smith-Hurd 1966) (repealed 1980, P.A. 81-1216, § 10-108).

11. U.S. Constitution, amend. V, XIV.

12. Pub. Utilities Comm'n v Pollak, 343 U.S. 451 (1952); Shelley v Kraemer, 334 U.S. 1 (1948).

13. McGuane v Chenango Court, Inc., 431 F.2d 1189 (2d Cir. 1970), *cert. denied,* 401 U.S. 994 (1971).

14. Weigand v Afton View Apartments, 473 F.2d 545 (8th Cir. 1973); Falzarano v United States, 607 F.2d 506 (1st Cir. 1979).

15. Geneva Towers Tenants Organization v Federated Mortgage Investors, 504 F.2d 483, 487 (9th Cir. 1974); Joy v Daniels, 479 F.2d 1236, 1239 (4th Cir. 1973); Owens v Housing Auth., 394 F. Supp. 1267, 1272-73 (D. Conn. 1975); Dew v McLendon Gardens Ass'n, 394 F. Supp. 1223, 1230 (N.D. Ga. 1975); Bloodworth v Oxford Village Townhouses, Inc., 377 F. Supp. 709, 716-17 (N.D. Ga. 1974); Anderson v Denny, 365 F. Supp. 1254, 1256 (W.D. Va. 1973). *See* Fenner v Bruce Manor, Inc., 409 F. Supp. 1332, 1343 (D. Md. 1976). *Contra,* Rodriguez v Towers Apartments, Inc., 416 F. Supp. 304 (D. P.R. 1976).

16. Lopez v Henry Phipps Plaza South, Inc., 498 F.2d 937, 943 (2d Cir. 1974); Male v Crossroads Assoc, 469 F.2d 616, 620–21 (2d Cir. 1972); McQueen v Druker, 438 F.2d 781 (1st Cir. 1971); Short v Fulton Redevelopment Co., 390 F. Supp. 517 (S.D. N.Y. 1975); McClellan v Univ. Heights, Inc., 338 F. Supp. 374 (D. R.I. 1972); Colon v Tompkins Square Neighbors, Inc., 294 F. Supp. 134 (S.D. N.Y. 1968).

17. Girard v 94th St. & Fifth Ave. Corp., 530 F.2d 66, 69 (2d Cir.), *cert. denied*, 425 U.S. 974 (1976); Joy v Daniels, *supra* note 15, at 1239; Weigand v Afton View Apartments, *supra* note 14; Lavoie v Bigwood, 457 F.2d 7 (1st Cir. 1972); McGuane v Chenango Court, Inc., *supra* note 13; Fallis v Dunbar, 386 F. Supp. 1117, 1120 (N.D. Ohio 1974), *aff'd*, 532 F.2d 1061 (6th Cir. 1976); Mullarkey v Borglum, 323 F. Supp. 1218, 1224 (S.D. N.Y. 1970); Langley v Monumental Corp., 496 F. Supp. 1144 (D. Md. 1980).

18. Lindsey v Normet, 405 U.S. 56 (1972).

19. Shelley v Kraemer, 334 U.S. 1 (1948).

20. Flagg Bros., Inc. v Brooks, 436 U.S. 149, 160 n.10 (1978).

Consistent with this principle, two courts of appeal have held that there is no state action in the foreclosure of a mortgage by the exercise of private, extrajudicial powers of sale pursuant to a provision of the mortgage instrument, even though a statute regulates such powers of sale. Warren v Gov't Nat'l Mortgage Ass'n, 611 F.2d 1229 (8th Cir. 1980), *cert. denied*, 101 S.Ct. 133 (1980); Roberts v Cameron-Brown Co., 556 F.2d 356 (5th Cir. 1977).

21. Carey v Population Services Int'l, 431 U.S. 678 (1977).

22. Moore v City of East Cleveland, 431 U.S. 494 (1977) (plurality opinion); *see* Smith v Organization of Foster Families for Equality and Reform, 431 U.S. 816 (1977).

23. The Fourteenth Amendment applies only to states, but the due process clause of the Fifth Amendment has been held to contain an implicit right of equal protection applicable to action by the federal government. Hampton v Wong, 426 U.S. 88 (1976).

24. Zablocki v Redhail, 434 U.S. 374 (1978); Carey v Population Services Int'l, *supra* note 21; San Antonio Ind. School Dist. v Rodriguez, 411 U.S. 1 (1973).

25. Maher v Roe, 432 U.S. 464 (1977).

26. White Egret Condominium v Franklin, 379 So.2d 346 (Fla. 1979).

The court held, however, that a child-exclusion policy must not be applied capriciously. In the case in question, because other children under the age of twelve were living in the condominium complex, the court held that the policy could not be enforced.

27. The guarantees of due process and equal protection require the existence of state action, but the court did not specify the basis for state action here. The lower appellate court found government action in the use of the courts by the condominium to enforce the child-exclusion policy. White Egret Condominium v Franklin, 358 So.2d 1084 (Fla. Dist. Ct. App. 1977).

28. White Egret Condominium v Franklin, 379 So.2d at 351.

29. Maher v Roe, *supra* note 25.
30. Dandridge v Williams, 397 U.S. 471 (1970).
31. Bynes v Toll, 512 F.2d 252 (2d Cir. 1975).
32. *Id.* at 225. See also Lamont Bldg. Co. v Court, 70 N.E.2d 447, 448 (Ohio 1946). Here, an apartment lease excluding children was held not to prohibit childbearing.
33. Taxpayers Ass'n v Weymouth Township, 364 A.2d 1016 (N.J. 1976), *appeal dismissed,* 430 U.S. 977 (1977); Shepard v Woodland Township Comm. & Planning Bd., 364 A.2d 1005 (N.J. 1976); Campbell v Barraud, 394 N.Y.S.2d 909 (App. Div. 1977). *Cf.* Maldini v Ambro, 330 N.E.2d 403 (N.Y. 1975), *appeal dismissed,* 423 U.S. 993 (1975); in this case a zoning amendment to establish a retirement community was upheld as a reasonable exercise of zoning power.
34. Mass. Bd. of Retirement v Murgia, 427 U.S. 307, 313 (1976).
35. For example, the Internal Revenue Code Provides a tax credit for expenses for child care and household services where the expenses are incurred to enable the taxpayer to work. The tax credit is 20 percent of the expenses, up to a maximum of $2,000 for one dependent child under fifteen years of age and a maximum of $4,000 for two or more dependent children. I.R.C. § 44A. In addition, a taxpayer can currently deduct $1,000 for each dependent child in determining taxable income. I.R.C. § 151(e), 152(a).

Another example is in the area of public education, which is funded by all taxpayers but most directly benefits parents with children in the public schools. The average expenditure nationwide in public primary and secondary schools was $1,900 in 1978–79. Bureau of the Census, *supra* note 8, at 162.

36. Graham v Richardson, 403 U.S. 365, 376 (1971). The Court also indicated that a family-size classification does not seriously affect the constitutionally protected childbearing decision.
37. Government action is usually upheld in cases decided by the reasonable basis test. In reviewing thirty recent volumes of the *Federal Reporter Second Series,* the author found thirty cases in which the reasonable basis standard was used. The government won all but one of the cases.
38. 431 U.S. 494 (1977).
39. A fifth member of the Court joined the plurality that invalidated the ordinance, but he did so on the basis that the ordinance was not substantially related to the public health and safety and thus violated the Fifth Amendment proscription against taking property without a public purpose, just compensation, and due process.
40. There is no explicit statement by the plurality that it is using the strict test. However, the plurality states that the ordinance implicates the test applied in cases in which the compelling interest standard has been used. 431 U.S. at 499.
41. Molino v Mayor & Council of Borough of Glassboro, 116 N.J. Super. 195, 281 A.2d 401, 405-6 (1971).
42. Riley v Stoves, 22 Ariz. App. 223, 526 P.2d 747 (1974).

# III FERTILITY CONTROL POLICIES:
*Some Possibilities*

# 7 GOVERNMENT REGULATION OF SEXUAL RELATIONSHIPS

The three chapters of Part III examine measures that government might employ to reduce the number of births and to control the natural increase of the American population. The measures are not the only ones we might examine, but they are policies that legislators seem likely to consider. Formal measures expressly designed to control the rate of natural increase will probably be necessary because education regarding the population issue is of questionable effectiveness in changing attitudes toward population growth.[1] Moreover, even if education had an important effect, attitudes do not appear capable of generating conduct or plans leading to a family size of less than two children. That is, concern with population growth affects childbearing decisions within the range of two to four children—the range that our society defines as acceptable and normal[2]—but not below that range.[3] An immediate cessation of population growth, however, requires a decline in family size to a level close to one child per couple.[4] A prompt halt to natural increase is therefore likely to necessitate the development of formal measures to reduce childbearing.

This chapter considers the constitutional aspects of government regulation of heterosexual relationships. To the extent that government can regulate the occurrence of heterosexual intercourse, it can affect the birth rate. Two general approaches are possible. First, even if marriage is not the only condition in which sexual intercourse is legally permissible, the vast majority of births result from sexual intercourse within marriage.[5] At the same time, the age at which couples marry affects the number of children they are likely to have; the younger the age at which marriage takes place, the larger the average family size.[6] By establishing a minimum age for marriage, a state thus can potentially influence the fertility rate. Accordingly, we must consider whether government can raise the minimum age for access to the social institution in which sexual relationships generate most births.

There is a second approach that government might pursue. The power of government to protect the public welfare may allow it to deter nonmarital sexual intercourse and cohabitation among young adults. The deterrent effect on births is potentially significant because of the growing incidence of sexual relationships among unmarried young adults. For instance, in 1979 there were 274,000 unmarried childless couples living together where at least one member was under twenty-five years of age; in 1970 the number was just 29,000.[7] If illegitimacy were to become socially acceptable, perhaps because the minimum age for marriage was substantially increased, cohabiting childless couples could become the source of considerable childbearing. Although their numbers currently are small in comparison to the number of married couples of the same age,[8] research shows the numbers rising at an impressive rate:

> Rarely does social change occur with such rapidity. Indeed, there have been few developments relating to marriage and family life which have been as dramatic as the rapid increase in unmarried cohabitation.[9]

Another indication of the incidence of nonmarital intercourse among young adults is that in 1976, three out of five women had experienced premarital sexual relations by age nineteen, and one out of five had become pregnant; both rates were higher than the rates five years earlier.[10] One result of nonmarital intercourse among young adults is that unmarried women under twenty years of age now account for 7 percent of all births.[11]

## ESTABLISHMENT OF A MINIMUM AGE FOR MARRIAGE

The first question to consider is whether states have constitutional authority to alter the minimum age at which individuals can enter marriage and thus undertake sexual relationships in the societal arrangement from which most births result. Probably the most important Supreme Court opinion relevant to the issue is *Zablocki v Redhail,* which was decided in 1978.[12] The case arose from a state statute that required an individual wanting to marry to obtain court permission before doing so if he/she was the parent of a minor child not in his/her custody and was under court order to support the child. Under the statute, court permission to marry could be obtained only if the individual had been meeting his/her child support obligation and only if the child was not, and was not likely to become, a public charge. In responding to a challenge to the statute, the Court noted that the protection of individual liberty contained in the due process clauses of the Constitution creates a fundamental right of privacy that shields decisions to marry.[13] The Court found a serious intrusion on the right of privacy because many individuals classified as needing court permission to marry would be unable to satisfy the statutory prerequisites for permission, while others so classified, even though they were able to meet the statutory prerequisites, would have their freedom of action regarding marriage severely hampered. Any serious state interference with marriage is constitutional only if the government is able to demonstrate that a compelling interest exists for its action and that its means are carefully constructed so as to advance only this interest.[14] That test, the Court concluded was not met here. However, while invalidating the statute in question, the Court pointed out that not all restrictions on the ability of individuals to marry are subject to the compelling interest test:

> By reaffirming the fundamental character of the right to marry, we do not mean to suggest that every state regulation which relates in any way to the incidents of or prerequisites for marriage must be subjected to rigorous scrutiny. To the contrary, reasonable regulations that do not significantly interfere with decisions to enter into the marital relationship may legitimately be imposed.[15]

That is, where the regulation of marriage does not directly and substantially burden decisions to marry and hence does not seriously infringe on the right of privacy, the action of government need only possess a reasonable basis to be constitutional.[16]

### Minimum Age and the Right of Privacy

The question arises whether a statute establishing a minimum marriage age seriously intrudes on the right of privacy. States have enacted such statutes, with the minimum age usually set at sixteen to eighteen years.[17] Could the statutes be required to satisfy the compelling interest standard on the ground that, by prohibiting marriage until a particular age, they directly and substantially burdened decisions to marry? For two reasons, it is unlikely that a serious intrusion on the right of privacy would be found in the statutes. First, the Court has emphasized that the states traditionally have had broad powers to regulate the conditions under which marriage can occur.[18] The compelling interest test is less likely to be applied to topics over which state legislatures by tradition exercise considerable authority.[19] Second, sexual activity among young people can constitutionally be subject to greater restrictions than sexual activity among adults because a greater burden is needed for a finding that a serious infringement exists on the right of privacy in the case of young people.[20] Regulation of the minimum age for marriage among young adults should be treated no differently, it can be argued, than regulation of their sexual activity,[21] and statutes now in force that establish minimum ages of less than twenty years for marriage should not violate the right of privacy. If existing statutes specifying a minimum marriage age do not infringe on the right of privacy, they will be constitutional as long as they possess a reasonable basis and promote a legitimate governmental objective.[22] A state can attempt to prevent immature persons from marrying, and a minimum age of less than twenty is a reasonable means for doing so.

## Raising Minimum Age to Curb Population Growth

Statutes that raised the minimum marriage age in order to curb population growth might possibly be held to directly and substantially burden decisions regarding marriage and to seriously infringe on the right of privacy, especially since the mandated age would have to be set at approximately twenty-five in order to significantly reduce childbearing.[23] Opponents can argue that a new minimum age set in the mid-twenties will severely discourage marriage decisions; the age by which half of all Americans now undertake their first marriage is roughly twenty-one for women and twenty-three for men.[24] A statute precluding marriage at the ages when marriage decisions are normally made is arguably a substantial burden on the decisions. *Zablocki,* however, does not necessarily support the argument. The statute in *Zablocki* was invalidated under the equal protection clause, which places restrictions on the development of classifications, rather than under the due process clause.[25] Use of the equal protection clause suggests that the statute was held unconstitutional because it distinguished a class of persons from the general population and imposed requirements for marriage on that class that did not have to be satisfied by anyone else. The unconstitutionality of the burdens placed on marriage thus seems to have resulted from grossly uneven requirements for marriage between classes of individuals rather than from the requirements as such.[26] The fundamental right impaired by the statute emanated from the due process clause, but the failing of the statute seems to have been the existence of substantial prerequisites to the exercise of the right that were applicable only to the members of one designated class of persons.

If this line of reasoning is correct, a serious infringement on the right of privacy does not normally result from restrictions on marriage that are placed on all individuals equally, unless couples are permanently denied access to marriage.[27] A uniform marriage age of twenty-five should thus be tested on the grounds of whether it is reasonably related to a proper governmental purpose, since virtually all persons who reach sexual maturity live to the age of twenty-five and therefore essentially no one would be denied access to marriage. The elimination of the serious problems stemming from population pressures might readily be viewed as a legitimate objective of government in its role of promoter of the public welfare. The social science research on which the new marriage age was based would seem to be sufficient to establish the age as a reasonable means to further the government's objective.

A minimum marriage age of twenty-five could possibly be held to intrude seriously on the right of privacy and hence could be required to satisfy the compelling interest standard. If so, the new minimum age would probably not be upheld. While the judiciary might see the control of population as a compelling governmental interest in light of the serious ramifications of population pressures, it is still questionable whether a substantial increase in the minimum marriage age satisfies the constitutional requirement that the increase be the narrowest possible means to control the number of births. A change in the age for marriage is an indirect way to reduce childbearing; research has found that the age of parents when their first child is born is a far more important factor in influencing completed family size.[28] Moreover, the higher age for marriage might not appreciably inhibit childbearing, because couples unable to marry might simply have their children out of wedlock.[29] The Court might therefore view an increase in the minimum marriage age as less well suited to the control of the birth rate than other measures that could be devised.

## REGULATION OF NONMARITAL RELATIONSHIPS

The issue of whether a state can establish a minimum marriage age and thus regulate the ability of couples to engage in sexual intercourse within the social institution in which most children are conceived is distinct from the issue of whether a state can regulate sexual intercourse outside marriage. The focus of our inquiry is sexual intercourse between persons of opposite sexes who are not married to one another and who have intercourse entirely in private and with mutual consent; our concern is not with "unnatural" sexual activities but with "normal" copulation. Thus, we omit from consideration court decisions regarding government regulation of sodomy and situations in which sexual intercourse stemmed from duress, fraud, or other factors negating consent.[30] Our focus, in short, is on the constitutionality of government regulation of nonmarital heterosexual intercourse under the conditions where most out-of-wedlock conceptions occur.[31]

The U.S. Supreme Court has not defined the extent to which government can regulate sexual relationships that occur in private and that involve individuals not married to each other.[32] The clearest indication of the direction in which constitutional philosophy is heading in this regard comes from the highest state courts of New Jersey and Iowa, both of which have held that government cannot prohibit such relationships or impose criminal sanctions on them.[33] In terms of delineating the rationale for its decision, the opinion of the New Jersey court is the better written. The court began by noting that, from the guarantee of liberty in the due process clauses, the Supreme Court had inferred a fundamental right of privacy protecting decisions whether to have a child. The New Jersey court advanced the principle that the right is concerned with individual freedom in general and that childbearing decisions are simply one aspect of this freedom. Since the Constitution protects the autonomy of the individual, the court held that a statute prohibiting sexual relationships between unmarried individuals that are carried on privately and that have no significant public consequences seriously infringed on the right of privacy. The statute was unconstitutional because it could not meet the compelling interest test. Although the court acknowledged that a compelling government interest might exist in preventing the spread of venereal disease and the birth of illegitimate children, the court did not view the statute as effective in deterring the sexual relationships leading to such consequences. Furthermore, the court did not view the prevention of sexual intercourse outside wedlock as a legitimate means for government to promote the institution of marriage and to protect public morals:

> [T]his statute can in no way be considered a permissible means of fostering what may otherwise be a socially beneficial institution. If we were to hold that the State could attempt to coerce people into marriage, we would undermine the very independent choice which lies at the core of the right of privacy. We do not doubt the beneficent qualities of marriage, both for individuals as well as for society as a whole. Yet, we can only reiterate that

decisions such as whether to marry are of a highly personal nature; they neither lend themselves to official coercion or sanction, nor fall within the regulatory power of those who are elected to govern.

This is not to suggest that the State may not regulate, in an appropriate manner, activities which are designed to further public morality. Our conclusion today extends no further than to strike down a measure which has as its objective the regulation of *private* morality. . . .

Fornication may be abhorrent to the morals and deeply held beliefs of many persons. But any appropriate "remedy" for such conduct cannot come from legislative fiat. Private personal acts between two consenting adults are not to be lightly meddled with by the State. The right of personal autonomy is fundamental to a free society. Persons who view fornication as opprobrious conduct may seek strenuously to dissuade people from engaging in it. However, they may not inhibit such conduct through the coercive power of the criminal law. As aptly stated by Sir Francis Bacon, "[t]he sum of behavior is to retain a man's own dignity without intruding on the liberty of others." The fornication statute mocks the dignity of both offenders and enforcers. Surely police have more pressing duties than to search out adults who live a so-called "wayward" life. Surely the dignity of the law is undermined when an intimate personal activity between consenting adults can be dragged into court and "exposed." More importantly, the liberty which is the birthright of every individual suffers dearly when the State can so grossly intrude on personal autonomy.[34]

The principle that the Constitution protects private sexual relationships outside marriage also appears in a line of cases involving the termination of government employees for undertaking extramarital relationships. The cases have most frequently involved personnel in public educational systems, and the courts have held that termination is not permitted unless the sexual relationships can be shown to impair the ability of the employees to carry out the duties of their positions or the ability of the educational systems to function effectively.[35] School systems have had considerable difficulty in terminating personnel under this standard,[36] even when pregnancy has resulted from the relationships,[37] unless a system could show that the relationship had a blatant impact on job performance.[38] In addition, the federal government was unable to terminate an Internal Revenue Service agent who had rented an apartment and carried on extramarital affairs while off duty; the government could show no apparent effect of the agent's activities upon his ability to perform his duties or upon the agency's ability to function.[39] On the other hand, two courts have reached opposite conclusions regarding whether police officers could be dismissed because of off-duty extramarital affairs that were conducted privately.[40] In the case in which termination was permitted, the affair was carried on with another police officer; in the case in which termination was prohibited, the affair was conducted with a woman who was not employed by the police department. The government interest in performance on duty and in the functioning of its police force was less likely to be endangered in the latter situation than in the former—a fact that may explain the different decisions reached by the two courts. In any event, the trend in court decisions suggests that government will generally be severely circumscribed in its ability to deter its employees, including police, from sexual relationships outside marriage. Government-mandated termination of employment for workers in the private sector, who comprise more than four-fifths of the labor force,[41] would be even more questionable as a means for deterring nonmarital sexual relationships.[42]

Government regulation of sexual relationships—raising the age for marriage or prohibiting sexual relationships among individuals who are not married to one another—evidently carries significant practical and constitutional limitations. Even if a substantially higher marriage age were to be constitutionally valid, it might simply encourage illegitimacy; moreover, the higher age is likely to curtail childbearing less than is a measure designed to delay the age at which couples have their first child. Prohibitions against, and sanctions imposed for, sexual relationships involving unmarried persons must satisfy the compelling interest standard. Since the prohibitions and sanctions would regulate sexual activity directly and childbearing only indirectly, they would probably not be the narrowest possible means of controlling fertility and would therefore be constitutionally dubious as a population policy. Furthermore, if such prohibitions were deemed constitutionally invalid, an increase in illegitimacy would probably follow imposition of a higher age for marriage. Population control, in short, appears to require other measures than government regulation of sexual relationships.

# NOTES

1. Patrick Jobes, *An Empirical Study of Short-Term Mass Communication Saturation and Perception of Population Problems,* 9 Journal of Sex Research 342 (1973).
2. Judith Blake, *Can We Believe Recent Data on Birth Expectations in the United States?,* 11 Demography 25 (1974); Judith Blake, *Ideal Family Size Among White Americans: A Quarter of a Century's Evidence,* 3 Demography 154 (1966).
3. Charles Westoff & James McCarthy, *Population Attitudes and Fertility,* 11 Family Planning Perspectives 93 (1979); David Kruegel, *Further Comment on J. Blake's "Can We Believe Recent Data on Birth Expectations in the United States?",* 12 Demography 157, 159 (1975); Larry Barnett, *Zero Population Growth, Inc.: A Second Study,* 6 Journal of Biosocial Science 1, 13-15 (1974). *See generally* A. Regula Herzog, Jerald Bachman, & Lloyd Johnston, "Concern for Others and Its Relationship to Specific Attitudes on Race Relations, Sex Roles, Ecology, and Population Control" (Survey Research Center, Institute for Social Research, University of Michigan, January, 1978), at table 8; Larry Barnett, *U.S. Population Growth as an Abstractly Perceived Problem,* 7 Demography 53 (1970).
4. Tomas Frejka, *Demographic Paths to a Stationary Population: The U.S. in International Comparison,* in Demographic and Social Aspects of Population Growth 623, 633 (Vol. I of the Research Reports of the U.S. Commission on Population Growth & the American Future, Charles F. Westoff & Robert Parke, Jr., eds.; Washington, D.C.: U.S. Gov't. Printing Office, 1972).
5. National Center for Health Statistics, U.S. Department of Health & Human Services, Trends and Differentials in Births to Unmarried Women: United States, 1970-76 (Vital & Health Statistics Series 21, No. 36; Washington, D.C.: U.S. Gov't. Printing Office, 1980). The study estimates that in 1972 the proportion of first births conceived out of wedlock was 22 percent among whites. *Id.* at 13. For all births, the proportion was probably lower. *See id.* at 18. Among some subgroups, however, a majority of births are conceived outside marriage. The study found that 60 percent of first births to nonwhites in 1972 were conceived out of wedlock. *Id.* at 13. Other research indicates that three-fourths of all births to women 15 to 19 years of age are the result of conceptions occurring outside marriage. Melvin Zelnik & John Kantner, *First Pregnancies to Women Aged 15-19: 1976 and 1971,* 10 Family Planning Perspectives 11, 17 (1978).
6. Larry Bumpass & Edward Mburugu, *Age at Marriage and Completed Family Size,* 24 Social Biology 31 (1977); Glen Elder & Richard Rockwell, *Marital Timing in Women's Life Patterns,* 1 Journal of Family History 34 (1976).
7. Bureau of the Census, U.S. Department of Commerce, *Marital Status and Living Arrangements: March 1979,* Current Population Reports, Series P-20, No. 349, at 4 (1980).

8. *Id.* at 7.

9. Paul Glick & Graham Spanier, *Married and Unmarried Cohabitation in the United States,* 42 Journal of Marriage & the Family 19, 20 (1980).

10. Melvin Zelnik, Young Kim, & John Kantner, *Probabilities of Intercourse and Conception among U.S. Teenage Women, 1971 and 1976,* 11 Family Planning Perspectives 177, 183 (1979).

11. *See* Bureau of the Census, U.S. Department of Commerce, Statistical Abstract of the United States: 1980, 101st ed., 61, 66 (Washington, D.C.: U.S. Gov't. Printing Office, 1980).

12. 434 U.S. 374 (1978).

13. The due process clauses prohibit government from depriving a person "of life, liberty, or property, without due process of law." Both the Fifth and Fourteenth Amendments contain such clauses; the former applies to the federal government and the latter applies to states and their subdivisions.

14. Roe v Wade, 410 U.S. 113 (1973).

15. 434 U.S. at 386.

16. *Id.* at 387; Califano v Jobst, 434 U.S. 47 (1977).

17. Homer H. Clark, Jr., The Law of Domestic Relations in the United States 78 (St. Paul, Minn.: West, 1968).

18. Sosna v Iowa, 419 U.S. 393, 404 (1975).

19. San Antonio Ind. School Dist. v Rodriguez, 411 U.S. 1, 40 (1973).

20. Carey v Population Services Int'l, 431 U.S. 678, 693 n.15, 703-7 (1977).

21. *See* Zablocki v Redhail, 434 U.S. 374, 386 (1978).

22. San Antonio Ind. School Dist., *supra* note 19, at 44.

23. Bumpass & Mburugu, *supra* note 6.

24. Bureau of the Census, *supra* note 11, at 83.

25. The equal protection clause of the Fourteenth Amendment provides that a state shall not "deny to any person within its jurisdiction the equal protection of the laws." While there is no express equal protection provision applicable to the federal government, one has been inferred from the due process clause of the Fifth Amendment. Hampton v Wong, 426 U.S. 88 (1976). See note 13, *supra.*

26. *See* Zablocki v Redhail, *supra* note 21, at 387.

27. *See* Loving v Virginia, 388 U.S. 1, 12 (1967).

28. Bumpass & Mburugu, *supra* note 6.

29. *Cf.* Murray Gendell, *Sweden Faces Zero Population Growth,* 35 Population Bulletin 1, 14, 17 (June, 1980). The median age at first marriage and the proportion of all births that are illegitimate are substantially higher in Sweden than in the United States, which suggests that factors delaying marriage tend to increase illegitimacy.

30. Criminal sanctions can be imposed on males who engage in sexual intercourse with females who are less than eighteen years of age even if the latter agree to the intercourse; a state can prohibit females under eighteen years old from giving effective consent to sexual relations. Michael M. v Superior Court of Sonoma County, 101 S.Ct. 1200 (1981).

31. Extramarital heterosexual intercourse that occurs in a commercial setting will also not be considered. Its prohibition, however, appears to be constitutional. J.B.K., Inc. v Caron, 600 F.2d 710 (8th Cir. 1979).

32. Carey v Population Services Int'l, *supra* note 20, at 694 n.17 (plurality opinion). *See also* Doe v Commonwealth's Attorney, 403 F.Supp. 1199 (E.D. Va. 1975) (three-judge court), *aff'd without opinion,* 425 U.S. 901 (1976).

33. State v Saunders, 75 N.J. 200, 381 A.2d 333 (1977); State v Pilcher, 242 N.W.2d 348 (Iowa 1976). *Accord,* People v Onofre, 424 N.Y.S.2d 566 (App. Div. 1980).

34. 381 A.2d at 342–43.

35. *E.g.,* Jerry v Bd. of Educ., 364 N.Y.S.2d 440, 324 N.E.2d 106 (1974).

36. *Compare* Thompson v Southwest School Dist., 483 F.Supp. 1170 (W.D. Mo. 1980) *and* Bd. of Trustees v Holso, 584 P.2d 1009 (Wyo. 1978) *with* Sullivan v Meade Ind. School Dist., 387 F.Supp. 1237 (D. S.D. 1975), *aff'd,* 530 F.2d 799 (8th Cir. 1976).

37. Andrews v Drew Mun. Separate School Dist., 507 F.2d 611 (5th Cir. 1975), *cert. dismissed,* 425 U.S. 559 (1976); Drake v Covington County Bd. of Educ., 371 F.Supp. 974 (M.D. Ala. 1974) (three-judge court); Lewis v Delaware State College, 455 F.Supp. 239 (D. Del. 1978).

38. Sedule v Capital School Dist., 425 F.Supp. 552 (D. Del. 1976), *aff'd,* 565 F.2d 153 (3d Cir. 1977), *cert. denied,* 434 U.S. 1039 (1978); Johnson v San Jacinto Jr. College, 498 F.Supp. 555, 573–77 (1980).

39. Major v Hampton, 413 F.Supp. 66 (E.D. La. 1976).

40. Shuman v City of Philadelphia, 470 F.Supp. 449 (E.D. Pa. 1979); Wilson v Swing, 463 F.Supp. 555 (M.D. N.C. 1978).

41. Bureau of the Census, *supra* note 11, at 411.

42. *See* United States Civil Serv. Comm'n v Nat'l Ass'n of Letter Carriers, 413 U.S. 548, 564 (1973).

# 8 TAXATION AND THE CONTROL OF FERTILITY

The simplest and most effective approach to curtailing fertility in the United States may be the use of financial incentives imposed by means of congressional powers of taxation. The economic cost of children is one of the most important determinants—if not the most important—of family size, and its impact is substantial.[1] The vast majority of American families are in income brackets in which taxation can have an important influence on the cost of children; in 1978, for instance, three out of four families with zero, one, or two children at home had incomes of at least $10,000.[2] Since the federal government has developed a relatively efficient and effective tax collection system, with whose procedures the public is well acquainted, manipulation of tax levels to curtail childbearing is likely to be highly effective.

Can Congress use its powers of taxation to influence the birth rate? The basic authority for taxing and spending stems from Article I, Section 8 of the Constitution. The relevant portion reads as follows:

> The Congress shall have power to lay and collect taxes, duties, imposts, and excises, to pay the debts and provide for the common defence and general welfare of the United States.

Congress thus possesses the authority to impose taxes and to spend the resulting revenues for the protection of the general welfare.[3] Hence, we must ask whether the concept of the general welfare can include population control. The Supreme Court has concluded that Congress has the power to determine the elements of the general welfare and that the judiciary will not overturn a congressional decision unless there is evidence that the legislators' judgment is arbitrary and clearly erroneous.[4] Congress thus has considerable latitude under its authority to promote the general welfare. Two additional factors increase the scope of congressional authority even further. First, the concept of the general welfare has been defined as an evolving one whose content changes with time.[5] Second, Article I, Section 8 of the Constitution provides Congress with the authority to "make all laws which shall be necessary and proper for carrying into execution the foregoing powers"; this gives the power to tax and spend for the general welfare a thrust the Court has called "quite expansive."[6] Since population pressures can threaten the quality of life and the standard of living, taxation and expenditures for the purpose of curbing the birth rate seem readily justifiable.[7]

## FORMS OF TAXATION TO REDUCE POPULATION GROWTH

The structure of a taxation system to reduce the birth rate can assume many different forms. It can include rewards for having no more than a certain number of children, penalties for having more than a certain number, or a combination of rewards and penalties. The goal of population control would be particularly well served if the incentives employed strongly discouraged births among young adults. In recent years, approximately one out of seven women has had a child prior to reaching her twentieth birthday, and one out of three has had a child prior to reaching her twenty-second birthday.[8] Reduction of these rates will contribute to population stabilization in two ways. First, research indicates that the later the age at which women bear their first child, the smaller their families will be.[9] Indeed, a woman's age at first giving birth has a substantially stronger relationship to completed family size than does a woman's age at marriage.[10] Second, reducing the incidence of early childbearing will raise the average age at which women have children and thus decrease the number of generations per century. The number of generations passing through a society in a given period of time directly affects the level of population growth. The median age of childbearing among mothers who have recently completed their childbearing period has fluctuated at around thirty.[11] An average age of thirty for having children will produce 3.3 generations per century; an average age of thirty-five will produce only 2.9 generations. All else being equal, population growth is 14 percent less in the latter situation.

Tax Surcharge for Childbearing

Different approaches can be used to structure a tax system that will reduce the number of births, including those to young adults. In examining some relevant provisions of the complex federal tax system, we confine our analysis to married couples, since less than 3 percent of all unmarried women bear children in any one year.[12] To minimize complexity, we consider tax levels only where the standard deduction is used.

Table 8.1 shows taxation levels for married couples who had zero, one, or two dependent children and who filed joint income tax returns for 1980.[13] Several adjusted gross incomes from $10,000 to

Table 8.1. Taxation Levels for Married Couples Who Filed Joint Income Tax Returns for 1980

| Adjusted Gross Income | 0 Dependent Children Tax | % of Income | 1 Dependent Child Tax | % of Income | 2 Dependent Children Tax | % of Income |
|---|---|---|---|---|---|---|
| $10,000 | $ 698 | 7.0% | $ 530 | 5.3% | $ 370 | 3.7% |
| $15,000 | $1,630 | 10.9% | $1,420 | 9.5% | $1,238 | 8.3% |
| $20,000 | $2,739 | 13.7% | $2,499 | 12.5% | $2,260 | 11.3% |
| $25,000 | $4,050 | 16.2% | $3,770 | 15.1% | $3,490 | 14.0% |
| $30,000 | $5,585 | 18.6% | $5,265 | 17.6% | $4,945 | 16.5% |

$30,000 are used for illustration. The table gives both the amount of tax paid and the proportion of each income that the amount represents.

Because of the exemption allowance given for each dependent, taxes at each income level fall as the number of children increases. At the same time, progressively higher rates mean that the number of dollars paid in taxes rises more rapidly than income and pushes upward the proportion of income going to taxes as earnings increase. Tripling income from $10,000 to $30,000 for a couple with no children raises eightfold the amount of tax paid (from $698 to $5,585) and raises the proportion of income consumed by taxes by a factor of 2 1/2 (from 7.0 to 18.6 percent). In varying the tax rate by income level, the current tax structure significantly affects the proportion of income paid in taxes—a fact that has implications for a policy of fertility control. If the current structure is to be used as a foundation on which to establish incentives to reduce fertility within the middle class, the proportion of income that needs to be taken may have to be larger among married couples with lower incomes, because a smaller proportion of their earnings is spent on taxes. For example, married couples earning $30,000 are not as likely to have a second child if compelled to pay 20 percent of their income tax annually as a charge for having that child, especially if they are already paying a surcharge for their first child. A 20 percent surcharge for the second child would enlarge the share of their income taken by the federal government by more than 3 percentage points and would cost them approximately $1,000 per year. However, couples earning $10,000 will probably not be discouraged from having a second child by a 20 percent surcharge, because it would increase the portion of their income going to the federal government by less than 1 percentage point and would cost just $74 per year. Within the middle class, then, surcharge rates may have to increase as income declines.[14]

It appears that the financial cost of children as a limitation on family size increases in influence after the first child and that the magnitude of its influence remains relatively constant for two or more children.[15] Since immediate population stabilization requires a total fertility rate only slightly above 1.0,[16] a surcharge for childbearing can be expected to have its greatest impact on the second birth, the one that needs to be discouraged the most. The impact of the surcharge can probably be enhanced by setting it at one level for the first child and at a higher level for second and subsequent children.[17]

## Tax Incentives for Childless Young Adults

Any policy of fertility control should attempt to discourage parenthood among young adults, particularly those under twenty years of age. Approximately half of all women who bear their first child between ages fifteen and nineteen intended to become pregnant; of those who did not plan a pregnancy, few used contraception.[18] A strong incentive to delay childbearing until at least age twenty can deter women who intend to become pregnant and encourage the use of contraception among women who do not. However, a surcharge for having a child prior to age twenty may not be the most effective approach, since couples (or at least women) who have a child at a young age are more likely than those undertaking parenthood at a later age to live in households that receive welfare and have low incomes.[19] Thus, a surcharge imposed for early childbearing might prove uncollectable often enough so that its impact would be seriously attenuated. The reduction of births to young adults might be more effectively accomplished by positive reinforcement. For example, a credit toward the federal income tax liability might be given for childlessness and would probably lower the incidence of births among couples under the age of twenty. Childless couples could be permitted to calculate their tax as if they had two dependent children; thus, a couple earning $10,000 in 1980 would have had a tax saving of some $300 and would have reduced the share of their income going to taxes by more than 3 percentage points. The credit could continue as long as the couple had no children. A permanent credit would promote childlessness among young couples by providing them with a substantial tax saving at the very age when their income is lowest.[20] It would also encourage lifetime commitments to childlessness by fostering delays in childbearing and thus allowing couples time to develop a stronger attachment to the advantages of the child-free lifestyle.[21]

## CONSTITUTIONALITY OF A FERTILITY CONTROL TAX

Estimation of the exact levels of tax surcharges and credits required for an effective population policy is pointless at this time; the levels that would be effective today would probably not be effective when a fertility control policy was implemented. Moreover, the exact levels are not essential for our purposes; we can assess the constitutionality of the incentive system with reasonable accuracy by using only the general structure we have outlined.

The Constitution provides Congress with the authority to tax and contains two express rules regarding the exercise of that authority. First, revenues raised through "direct" and "capitation" taxes are to be obtained from sources within the states in proportion to the respective population numbers of the states.[22] Second, revenues to be raised through income taxes, though they may be direct taxes, need not be so apportioned.[23] If Congress imposes a direct or a capitation tax, it must establish the total revenue that it wants to obtain, determine from the census the proportion of the total population that resides in each state, and raise an amount from sources within each state that represents the proportion of the population residing there. Of the total revenue Congress raises, a direct or a capitation tax will therefore derive 5 percent from a state that has 5 percent of the population. However, apportionment among the states is not necessary for a tax levied on income; the revenue that Congress wants to obtain through an income tax can be secured without regard to the distribution of population numbers among the states.

### Classification of the Fertility Control Tax

To determine the type of levy that is imposed by the fertility control policy, we must ask whether the policy establishes an income tax; if it does, apportionment is not required. The Supreme Court has defined the term *income* as "the gain derived from capital, from labor, or from both combined"[24] and as "undeniable accessions to wealth, clearly realized, and over which the taxpayers have complete dominion."[25] Income, therefore, refers to the acquisition of economic assets, and the acquisition must be actual, not potential.[26] Given this definition, it appears unlikely that the fertility control policy can be construed as imposing a tax on income. Children entail a substantial economic loss, not a gain; indeed, in 1980 prices the direct maintenance costs of a child to age eighteen are estimated at between $48,000 and $73,000.[27] The fertility control policy thus has no relationship to an increase in wealth. Moreover, few Americans view children as even a potential economic asset,[28] and the Court has held that income must generally be defined in accordance with the manner in which it is understood in everyday life.[29]

An argument in favor of the fertility control policy as an income tax is that the policy establishes classifications by family size that affect the amount of tax owed, that the classifications are additions to an existing tax on income, and that they do not alter the nature of the tax.[30] The argument, however, appears to confuse the distinction between the subject of a levy and its measure. The subject is the phenomenon on which the levy is placed; the measure is the quantitative dimension against which the rate of the levy is applied to calculate the amount of money owed. Use of income as the measure of a levy does not mean that income is the subject.[31] The fertility control policy uses income to determine the amount a couple must pay for having had a child and thus makes income the measure of the levy. Income is not, and cannot be, the subject because children do not increase economic assets.

If the fertility control policy does not impose a tax on income, we must ascertain whether it establishes a direct tax or a capitation tax. A tax of either kind is subject to the requirement of apportionment. By definition, a *direct tax* is one imposed on property, and it "falls upon the owner merely because he is the owner, regardless of his use or disposition of the property."[32] The fertility control policy is unlikely to establish a direct tax, because the subject of its levy is childbearing, and the courts have never construed procreation as involving an interest in property. Indeed, the Supreme Court appears to have resisted the view that childbearing implicates property; the guarantee of due process from which constitutional protections for childbearing originate covers interests in both property and liberty, but the Court has used the interest in liberty to protect procreation.[33] If property as a legal dimension is not involved in childbearing, a levy to limit fertility would seem not to be a direct tax.

We are thus left with the question whether the fertility control policy imposes a *capitation tax* — that is, a fixed sum placed upon each person in the taxed class(es). While the sum may vary among demographic categories based, for instance, on age and sex, it is unaffected by wealth or property within each of the taxed classes.[34] A capitation tax is a tax "of a fixed amount upon all the persons, or upon all the persons of a certain class, within the jurisdiction of the taxing power, without regard to the amount of their property or the occupations or business in which they may be engaged."[35] A cogent argument can be made that the fertility control policy levies a capitation tax because the sum paid by couples is determined by the number of children they have. Under this argument, however, the subject of the levy is children. The argument overlooks the phenomenon that the levy is intended to affect — namely, the annual number of births. If the fertility control policy established a capitation tax, it would be taxing *children* in order to influence *childbearing* — two phenomena that, while related, are nonetheless distinct. In reality, the subject of the policy is childbearing, and the number of children that a married couple has had simply determines the rate to be applied to the measure of the tax (namely, income). This conclusion stems both from the purpose of the policy and from the inequitable result that would follow if the policy were held to create a capitation tax. The designation of the subject of a levy is influenced by whether the designation produces an equitable result.[36] If the fertility control policy imposed a capitation tax, apportionment would be required; but apportioning the tax would generate inequitable burdens, because the distribution of population among the states is not the same as the distribution of births.[37]

The fertility control policy, therefore, does not appear to establish an income tax, a direct tax, or a capitation tax. Does it create any of the other types of levies mentioned in Article I, Section 8 — namely, excises, duties, or imposts? An excise is a levy on the manufacture, sale, or use of an item or on the privilege of conducting business or engaging in an occupation.[38] A duty, like an impost, is a levy on the importation of an item, but a duty can also fall on the exportation or consumption of an item.[39] The fertility control policy clearly does not establish an excise, duty, or impost. Article I, Section 8 therefore includes no category for the fertility control levy and apparently cannot provide constitutional authority for the policy.

An argument might be advanced that the fertility control policy can be justified by a line of cases in which the Supreme Court has held a levy enacted under Article I, Section 8 is constitutional even though the levy regulated an activity and imposed a burden that made continuance of the activity difficult or impossible.[40] The fertility control policy would, of course, have a similar effect on childbearing. However, the Court in these cases has always considered levies that, while regulating an activity, could be included in one of the categories of Article I. The incentives established by the fertility control policy appear not to fall into any of the categories. Accordingly, the fact that Article I, Section 8 can be used to regulate an activity is of no assistance in establishing it as a constitutional foundation for the fertility control policy.

## Commerce Clause

If Article I, Section 8 does not provide Congress with the authority to adopt the fertility control policy because a tax as such is not involved, the policy can probably still be implemented under another provision of the Constitution. The commerce clause delegates to Congress the power "to regulate commerce with foreign nations, and among the several states,"[41] and it permits imposition of monetary levies to attain its goals. The Supreme Court has thus upheld a federal law that placed a charge on boat owners for each immigrant their boats brought to the United States.[42] The revenues were used to assist immigrants who encountered difficulties and to inspect arriving vessels so that criminals and people who were mentally ill or unable to support themselves could be identified and prevented from entering the country. The Court agreed that the charge was not a tax under Article I, Section 8 but added that this finding did not invalidate the charge. The statute was held to be appropriate legislation to accomplish a goal within the purview of the commerce clause: "If this is an expedient regulation of commerce by Congress, and the end to be attained is one falling within that power, the act is not void, because, within a loose and more extended sense than was used in the Constitution, it is called a tax."[43]

It appears probable that the commerce clause can be used to regulate population size. As we saw in chapter 2, population growth is creating serious problems that affect the national economy, and the Court has ruled that the clause provides Congress with considerable power to deal with the causes of such problems:

> The broad authority of Congress under the Commerce Clause has, of course, long been interpreted to extend beyond activities actually *in* interstate commerce to reach other activities that, while wholly local in nature, nevertheless substantially *affect* interstate commerce.[44]

For example, the Court has held that the commerce clause authorizes a federal statute establishing limits on the quantity of wheat grown on private farms and imposing monetary penalties on farmers for violations of the limits, even if the excess wheat was consumed solely on the farm.[45] The Court found that wheat was important to the national economy, that its supply relative to demand affected its price, and that the quantity of wheat consumed by the growers themselves was the most important variable in the amount of wheat that made its way to the market. Since the wheat grown and consumed by individual farmers had an appreciable effect on the supply and price of wheat and hence on commerce, the Court held that the statute in question was a legitimate exercise of the authority delegated to Congress by the commerce clause:

> The effect of the statute before us is to restrict the amount which may be produced for market and the extent as well to which one may forestall resort to the market by producing to meet his own needs. That appellee's own contribution to the demand for wheat may be trivial by itself is not enough to remove him from the scope of federal regulation where, as here, his contribution, taken together with that of many others similarly situated, is far from trivial.[46]

The commerce clause thus permits Congress to regulate the conduct of individuals whenever that conduct taken collectively has a significant impact on the national economy. Congressional regulation can include monetary incentives. A fertility control policy employing the income tax system appears to be readily subsumable under the principles of the commerce clause.

## Fertility Control and the Right of Privacy

While the commerce clause may allow tax incentives for fertility control, the policy may violate another provision of the Constitution and therefore be invalid.[47] The Court has held that the guarantee of liberty in the due process clauses of the Constitution creates a right of privacy that protects childbearing from unnecessary governmental interference.[48] Government action that seriously infringes on the right of privacy will be constitutional only if it advances a compelling interest and is no broader than necessary to achieve that interest. If no serious infringement exists, government need have no more than a reasonable basis for its action—a standard that is more easily met.[49] Would the fertility control policy seriously intrude on the right of privacy? Under the current state of constitutional law, the answer appears to be affirmative. The Supreme Court has indicated that the crucial factor in determining the existence of a serious infringement on the right of privacy is whether government has placed a direct and substantial burden on, and hence discouraged conduct protected by, the right. Direct negative reinforcement of protected conduct through use of significant financial penalties apparently would be a serious intrusion on the right of privacy; positive reinforcement through use of financial rewards to motivate individuals to pursue a certain course of protected conduct is not, even though the reinforcement may incidentally discourage other conduct that is also protected. The Court has therefore upheld a state regulation under which the costs of childbirth were paid for indigent women but the costs of abortions were not. The Court applied only the reasonable basis test because the regulation did not, in its view, directly burden access to abortions:

> The Connecticut regulation places no obstacles—absolute or otherwise—in the pregnant woman's path to an abortion. An indigent woman who desires an abortion suffers no disadvantage as a consequence of Connecticut's decision to fund childbirth; she continues as before to be dependent on private sources for the services she desires. The State may have made childbirth a more attractive alternative, thereby influencing the woman's decision, but it has imposed no restriction on access to abortions that was not already there. The indigency that may make it difficult—and in some cases, perhaps, impossible—for some women to have abortions is neither created nor in any way affected by the Connecticut regulation.[50]

At the same time the Court, in upholding a congressional restriction against the use of federal funds for abortions, pointed out that a penalty imposed directly on abortions would encounter a more serious constitutional hurdle:

> A substantial constitutional question would arise if Congress had attempted to withhold all Medicaid benefits from an otherwise eligible candidate simply because that candidate had exercised her constitutionally protected freedom to terminate her pregnancy by abortion. This would be analogous to *Sherbert v Verner,* where this Court held that a State may not . . . withhold *all* unemployment compensation benefits from a claimant who would otherwise be eligible for such benefits but for the fact that she is unwilling to work one day per week on her Sabbath.[51]

In imposing substantial financial penalties for childbearing, a fertility control policy employing the government's tax system will place a major burden directly on procreation and therefore will constitute a serious intrusion on the right of privacy. However, the policy is not thereby automatically unconstitutional; it may still survive if it can satisfy the strict compelling interest standard. Chapter 2 illustrated the serious problems emanating from excessive population numbers; dealing with the cause of the problems can readily be held to be a compelling government interest. Moreover, the financial incentives of the proposed policy seem not to be unnecessarily broad means for dealing with excessive childbearing. A fertility control policy that uses the federal tax system may thus be justified under the Constitution.[52]

## NOTES

1. Depending on the approach utilized and the number of children being considered, research indicates that financial cost is the most important reason for not having another child among 37 to 68 percent of American wives. Husbands do not appear to differ markedly from wives in this regard. Rodolfo Bulatao & Fred Arnold, *Relationships Between the Value and Cost of Children and Fertility: Cross-Cultural Evidence,* in 1 International Population Conference, Mexico, 1977 141, 146 (International Union for the Scientific Study of Population, 1977); Rodolfo Bulatao, *Values and Disvalues of Children in Successive Childbearing Decisions,* 18 Demography 1 (1981); "Attitudes about Children: Report to Respondents" (Survey Research Center, Institute for Social Research, University of Michigan, October 1976) at table 2.

2. Bureau of the Census, U.S. Department of Commerce, *Money Income of Families and Persons in the United States: 1978*, Current Population Reports, Series P-60, No. 123, at 112 (1980).
3. Nicol v Ames, 173 U.S. 509, 515 (1899).
4. Mathews v de Castro, 429 U.S. 181, 185 (1976); Helvering v Davis, 301 U.S. 619, 640 (1937).
5. Helvering v Davis, 301 U.S. 619, 641 (1937).
6. Buckley v Valeo, 424 U.S. 1, 90 (1976).
7. This reasoning applies not only to taxation to control the birth rate but also to the expenditure of revenues to induce states to implement tuition charges in the public schools, which is discussed in the next chapter.
8. Bureau of the Census, U.S. Department of Commerce, *Fertility of American Women: June 1979*, Current Population Reports, Series P-20, No. 358, at 61 (1980).
9. Sara Millman & Gerry Hendershot, *Early Fertility and Lifetime Fertility*, 12 Family Planning Perspectives 139 (1980).
10. Larry Bumpass & Edward Mburugu, *Age at Marriage and Completed Family Size*, 24 Social Biology 31 (1977).
11. Bureau of the Census, *supra* note 8, at 59.
12. National Center for Health Statistics, U.S. Department of Health & Human Services, Trends and Differentials in Births to Unmarried Women: United States, 1970-76 4, 37 (Vital & Health Statistics Series 21, No. 36; Washington, D.C.: U.S. Gov't. Printing Office, 1980).
13. Internal Revenue Service, Department of the Treasury, Instructions for Preparing Form 1040: 1980 34-37 (Washington, D.C.: U.S. Gov't. Printing Office, 1980).
14. The sum to be paid for the birth of a child might be determined by applying a given rate to taxable income or to the tax owed under the existing tax structure. The latter approach is used here and follows the suggestion of Edward H. Rabin, *Population Control Through Financial Incentives*, 23 Hastings Law Journal 1353 (1972).
15. Bulatao & Arnold, *supra* note 1; Bulatao, *supra* note 1, at 14.
16. Tomas Frejka, *Demographic Paths to a Stationary Population: The U.S. in International Comparison*, in Demographic and Social Aspects of Population Growth 623, 633 (Vol. I of the Research Reports of the U.S. Commission on Population Growth & the American Future, Charles F. Westoff & Robert Parke, Jr., eds., 1972).
17. Because there are economies of scale as family size increases, it may be necessary to raise the surcharge rates with each succeeding child. Edward Lazear & Robert Michael, "Family Size and the Distribution of Real Per Capita Income" (revised version of Working Paper No. 230 of the National Bureau of Economic Research, 1979). *See* Thomas Espenshade, *The Value and Cost of Children*, 32 Population Bulletin 1, 33 (April 1977).
18. Melvin Zelnik & John Kantner, *First Pregnancies to Women Aged 15-19: 1976 and 1971*, 10 Family Planning Perspectives 11, 16 (1978).

19. Kristin Moore, *Teenage Childbirth and Welfare Dependency*, 10 Family Planning Perspectives 233 (1978). *See* Josefina Card & L. Wise, *Teenage Mothers and Teenage Fathers: The Impact of Early Childbearing on the Parents' Personal and Professional Lives*, 10 Family Planning Perspectives 199 (1978).

20. Bureau of the Census, U.S. Department of Commerce, Statistical Abstract of the United States: 1980, 101st ed., 458 (Washington, D.C.: U.S. Gov't. Printing Office, 1980).

21. Jean E. Veevers, Childless by Choice 20-27 (Toronto: Butterworth, 1980).

22. Article I, Section 2 of the Constitution contains the following requirement: "Representatives and direct taxes shall be apportioned among the several states which may be included within this Union, according to their respective numbers [as determined by a census every ten years]." Article I, Section 9 provides: "No capitation, or other direct, tax shall be laid, unless in proportion to the census or enumeration herein before directed to be taken." An explanation of the reasons for and operation of these provisions appears in Pollock v Farmers Loan & Trust Co., 157 U.S. 429 (1895) and 158 U.S. 601 (1895).

23. The Sixteenth Amendment provides that "[t]he Congress shall have power to lay and collect taxes on incomes, from whatever source derived, without apportionment among the several States, and without regard to any census or enumeration." The amendment did not expand the taxing power of Congress; it simply eliminated the requirement that direct taxes be apportioned when levied on income. Eisner v Macomber, 252 U.S. 189, 205-6 (1920).

24. Eisner v Macomber, *supra* note 23, at 207.

25. Comm'r v Glenshaw Glass Co., 348 U.S. 426, 431 (1955).

26. United States v Safety Car Heating & Lighting Co., 297 U.S. 88, 99 (1936).

27. Thomas J. Espenshade, *Raising a Child Can Now Cost $85,000*, 8 Intercom 1, 11 (September, 1980).

28. Bulatao & Arnold, *supra* note 1, at 147; Bulatao, *supra* note 1, at table 1; "Attitudes about Children: Report to Respondents," *supra* note 1, at table 1; Lois Hoffman, Arland Thornton, & Jean Manis, *The Value of Children to Parents in the United States*, 1 Journal of Population 91, 97 (1978).

29. United States v Safety Car Heating and Lighting Co., *supra* note 26, at 99.

30. Rabin, *supra* note 14, at 1375. Rabin rejects the argument, but he does not give his reasons for doing so. *Id.* at 1376.

31. Flint v Stone Tracy Co., 220 U.S. 107, 165 (1911).

32. Fernandez v Weiner, 326 U.S. 340, 362 (1945).

33. Smith v Organization of Foster Families for Equality & Reform, 431 U.S. 816 (1977), *rev'g* 418 F. Supp. 277 (S.D. N.Y. 1976). *See generally* Bd. of Regents v Roth, 408 U.S. 564, 576-77 (1972).

34. Breedlove v Suttles, 302 U.S. 277, 281 (1937); Hamilton v People, 24 Colo. 301, 51 P. 425, 426 (1897).

TAXATION AND THE CONTROL OF FERTILITY 139

35. Thomas M. Cooley, 1 The Law of Taxation, 4th ed. 122 (Chicago: Callaghan, 1924).
36. *See* United Air Lines, Inc. v Mahin, 410 U.S. 623 (1973).
37. For example, if the levy had been in effect in 1978 and been apportioned, the residents of Oregon would have paid almost twice as much as the residents of Utah, even though each state had the same number of births. *See* Bureau of the Census, *supra* note 20, at 12, 63.
38. Flint v Stone Tracy Co., 220 U.S. 107, 151 (1911).
39. Cooley, *supra* note 35, at 73-75.
40. Fernandez v Wiener, 326 U.S. 340, 362 (1945); Sonzinsky v United States, 300 U.S. 506, 513 (1937); Veazie Bank v Fenno, 75 U.S. (8 Wall.) 533, 548 (1869).
41. U.S. Constitution, art. I, § 8, cl. 3.
42. Head Money Cases, 112 U.S. 580 (1884).
43. *Id.* at 596.
44. McLain v Real Estate Bd., 444 U.S. 232, 241 (1980).
45. Wickard v Filburn, 317 U.S. 111 (1942).
The limits and penalties were part of a program that farmers were not compelled to join, though there were financial incentives to participate. The fact of voluntary participation in the program does not affect the decision of the Court with regard to the commerce clause. Under the clause, Congress can impose absolute prohibitions on private conduct that is detrimental to the national economy. *E.g.,* United States v Darby, 312 U.S. 100 (1941); Katzenbach v McClung, 379 U.S. 294 (1964).
46. 317 U.S. at 127-28.
47. Nat'l League of Cities v Usery, 426 U.S. 833 (1976).
48. Carey v Population Services Int'l, 431 U.S. 678 (1977).
The due process clause of the Fifth Amendment is applicable to the federal government and provides that "[n]o person shall . . . be deprived of life, liberty, or property, without due process of law." The due process clause of the Fourteenth Amendment provides that "[n]o State shall . . . deprive any person of life, liberty, or property, without due process of law."
49. Zablocki v Redhail, 434 U.S. 374 (1978); Roe v Wade, 410 U.S. 113 (1973); Maher v Roe, 432 U.S. 464 (1977).
50. Maher v Roe, 432 U.S. 464, 474 (1977).
51. Harris v McRae, 100 S.Ct. 2671, 2688 n.19 (1980).
52. However, the policy probably cannot be applied to children born prior to its adoption, because a retroactive assessment would result. *See* Welch v Henry, 305 U.S. 134, 147 (1938).

# 9 TUITION IN THE PUBLIC SCHOOLS

If financial incentives are to be used to curtail the number of births and to control population numbers, we might consider other options. One possible approach would be a requirement that parents pay at least some portion of the cost of educating their children, a cost now borne by the public at large. The cost is not only substantial; it is increasing rapidly. In 1960 the average expenditure per pupil in public primary and secondary schools was $375; in 1970 it was $816; in 1979 it reached $1,900. The increased cost of education has been outpacing income; public schools have been taking from taxpayers an increasing proportion of their incomes. In 1960 the average expenditure per student constituted 17 percent of per capita personal income; by 1979 it constituted 22 percent.[1] Clearly, the public subsidy for education cannot continue to take an expanding share of income; sooner or later, the needs of education will exceed the ability or willingness of the public to provide funds. A decline in educational quality is the likely result. Charging tuition in the public schools might thus not only reduce the birth rate but also simultaneously protect an essential social service.

## CONSTITUTIONALITY OF TUITION CHARGES

Does the Constitution permit charges for public school tuition? The case most relevant to the question is *San Antonio Independent School District v Rodriguez,* decided by the Supreme Court in 1973.[2] At issue was a system of financing public schools whereby funds came largely from local property taxes. Under the system, poor localities generated smaller amounts of revenue than wealthy localities from a given rate of taxation and could match the revenue raised by the latter only if the poor communities imposed a substantially higher tax rate and thus used a larger share of their resources for education. Although a state program provided money that reduced the differences between localities in expenditures per student, the differences that remained were appreciable and resulted in a constitutional challenge to the use of local property taxation as a method of providing school funds. The challenge relied on two arguments. First, it was claimed that the system differentiated by wealth and thereby created a classification under the equal protection clause that was constitutionally suspect. Second, it was argued that education provided skills vital in modern society, and particularly skills vital to the constitutionally protected freedom of expression and the right to vote; that education was therefore a fundamental constitutional right; and that a financing system based on property taxes prevented the right from being equally available to all citizens. If the system established a suspect class or penalized a fundamental constitutional right, it would be valid only if it was shown to serve a compelling government interest and to be the narrowest possible means to achieve the interest. The Court, however, rejected both arguments, and as a result the financing system was required only to possess a reasonable basis. The Court found a reasonable basis in the fact that the system was well within the boundaries of accepted educational and financial policy and in the fact that the state was acting to extend educational services to its citizens rather than to withdraw them. The system was accordingly held to be constitutional.

The reasoning employed by the Court in this matter is important. The Court emphasized that the equal protection clause does not require individuals to be identical in terms of wealth or the opportunities wealth affords. As a result, the poor constitute a suspect class only if their poverty totally prevents them from paying for a government benefit and they are absolutely deprived of an opportunity to participate in the benefit. In the case in question, the challenge was brought against a system of financing a government benefit whose quality was claimed to be lower for children of the poor than for children of the wealthy. There was no argument that the poor were completely deprived of the benefit, and therefore the system did not make them a suspect class. Nonetheless, the Court added an important caveat:

> If elementary and secondary education were made available by the State only to those able to pay a tuition assessed against each pupil, there would be a clearly defined class of "poor" people—definable in terms of their inability to pay the prescribed sum—who would be absolutely precluded from receiving an education. That case would present a far more compelling set of circumstances for judicial assistance than the case before us today.[3]

While the poor cannot be charged a fee that prevents their children from acquiring an education in the public schools, a state is evidently not precluded from imposing a fee that varies according to the ability of parents to pay. When a state provides educational services, it need only make them equally available to all citizens.[4] It would seem to do so when it takes account of the financial resources of parents and charges only as much as they can afford. Accordingly, one federal court has held that a program that paid part of the tuition for handicapped children who had to attend private schools was invalid insofar as the program affected parents who were unable to provide the portion of tuition not paid by the program. The program was not required to pay the full tuition costs of all handicapped children attending private schools, but it was constitutionally compelled to pay whatever costs the parents could not.[5]

If tuition charges are not a fixed amount to be paid by everyone but are varied according to the parents' ability to pay, all children will be treated equally, no child will be prevented by the charges from attending the public schools, and the poor will not constitute a suspect class. As a result, the constitutionality of a tuition system requires only a reasonable basis insofar as wealth is concerned. However, even if a system of tuition creates no suspect class of indigent persons, the compelling interest test will still be employed if the system seriously interferes with a fundamental constitutional right. Before the strict test of constitutionality is used, there must be both (1) a fundamental constitutional right and (2) a direct and substantial interference with it.[6] The criteria, however, are evidently not satisfied by a variable tuition charge. In *San Antonio Independent School District* the Court concluded that education was not a fundamental right in spite of its undeniable importance to society and to the exercise of already established constitutional rights such as free expression and participation in elections:

> Education, of course, is not among the rights afforded explicit protection under our Federal Constitution. Nor do we find any basis for saying it is implicitly so protected. As we have said, the undisputed importance of education will not alone cause this Court to depart from the usual [i.e., reasonable basis] standard for reviewing a State's social and economic legislation.[7]

Even though education has not been deemed a fundamental right and therefore cannot bring the compelling interest test into use, another fundamental constitutional right may do so—namely, the right of privacy that protects childbearing. It may be argued that a tuition system seriously infringes on the right of privacy by discouraging large families. The argument, however, does not appear to be well founded. Tuition charges will be determined by the parents' ability to pay, taking into account income and expenses for essential items, and while the charges will undoubtedly increase the pressure on family finances and discourage childbearing, all children in a family will be able to attend the public schools regardless of their parents' financial circumstances. Moreover, payment of tuition charges will not begin until several years after a child's birth, and the delay will permit other factors to have an important effect on the parents' subsequent childbearing decisions. It is thus doubtful that tuition charges can be said to constitute a substantial burden on childbearing or to seriously intrude on the right of privacy.

A tuition system in the public schools can readily satisfy the test of reasonableness since it can be expected to discourage births by reducing the income that families have available to spend on discretionary items. A tuition system could also be structured to strengthen the incentive to limit childbearing. For example, tuition charges for education in essential skills could be determined by ability of middle- and upper-income parents to pay, but a single flat fee could be charged for advanced training. Thus, the fee for the first eight or ten years of school might be established on the basis of ability to pay, while the fee for further education might be set at a higher level and be unaffected by parental income. Since a tuition system would presumably not apply to children already born (or even conceived), such an approach would strengthen the motivation to limit childbearing to one or two children by utilizing society's emphasis on advanced education and the desire of parents in the middle and upper classes to have their children attend college. A dual level of tuition charges appears to be constitutionally valid. In *San Antonio Independent School District* the Court concluded that the Constitution does not obligate public schools to develop the talents of students to the fullest possible extent. This principle had led one Court of Appeals to hold that a school system is not constitutionally required to offer bilingual and bicultural education to students from Mexican and Indian backgrounds[8] or remedial instruction in English to Chinese-speaking students.[9] Government is obligated only to offer its educational services in a manner that makes them equally available to everyone, and students who suffer from handicaps that they cannot overcome with the opportunities afforded are not due special consideration. The court concluded:

> Every student brings to the starting line of his educational career different advantages and disadvantages caused in part by social, economic, and cultural backgrounds, created and continued completely apart from any contribution by the school system. That some of these may be impediments which can be overcome does not amount to a "denial" by the Board [of Education] of educational opportunities within the meaning of the Fourteenth Amendment should the Board fail to give them special attention.[10]

In line with this reasoning, students who are capable of benefiting from advanced education are not apparently entitled to it if they are unable to afford the tuition. This principle is consistent with the conclusion of the Supreme Court that the Constitution does not provide a right to a level of public financial assistance that will satisfy the minimum needs of the individual, let alone a level that will permit the individual to maximize his or her potential abilities.[11] Indeed, government can manipulate financial incentives in its programs in order to achieve certain desired goals as long as the goals are legitimate, and the manipulation of incentives is permissible even though important human needs may be affected.[12] At the same time, government can regulate the conditions under which its educational services are used, and the fact that some persons who are eligible for the services are not able to utilize them raises no constitutional problem if a reasonable basis exists for the regulations.[13] Accordingly, government can structure educational services in a manner that motivates individuals to have fewer children as long as the services are offered to all similarly situated persons on the same terms.

## CONGRESSIONAL ACTION TO ESTABLISH A TUITION SYSTEM

Primary and secondary schools are under the control of the states, not the federal government. If a tuition system is to have a substantial impact on the birth rate, it will have to exist in a majority of the states. Therefore, we must consider what action Congress can take to promote a tuition system. Two options are possible. First, Congress might require states to establish tuition systems as a condition for receiving federal financial assistance. Such a requirement can be expected to have an appreciable influence because 9 percent of the revenues for public primary and secondary education currently come from the federal government.[14] Congress can impose conditions upon the monies it gives to states as long as the conditions do not violate the Constitution;[15] as we have seen, a tuition system scaled according to ability to pay seems constitutionally valid.

Second, Congress might enact legislation that mandates the adoption of a tuition system by the states. This approach, however, presents a difficult constitutional issue; the authority of the federal government supersedes that of a state only in those areas in which the former may act. Congress cannot intrude on state functions without limitation; under the Tenth Amendment, "[t]he powers not delegated to the United States by the Constitution, nor prohibited by it to the States, are reserved to the States respectively, or to the people." States thus participate with the federal government in a system that assigns them certain powers with which Congress cannot interfere. While the federal government is supreme within its constitutionally authorized domain, the states are independent entities whose sovereignty cannot otherwise be impaired. Accordingly, the Supreme Court has held that Congress is constitutionally impotent to extend to the employees of state and local governments the standards that it has established for minimum wages and maximum working hours in private enterprise. Such an extension, the Supreme Court felt, would

> ... impermissibly interfere with the integral governmental functions of these bodies [because it would] significantly alter or displace the States' abilities to structure employer-employee relationships in such areas as fire prevention, police protection, sanitation, public health, and parks and recreation. These activities are typical of those performed by state and local governments in discharging their dual functions of administering the public law and furnishing public services. Indeed, it is functions such as these which governments are created to provide, services such as these which the States have traditionally afforded their citizens. If Congress may withdraw from the States the authority to make those fundamental employment decisions upon which their systems for performance of these functions must rest, we think there would be little left of the States' separate and independent existence.[16]

Education is clearly established as one of the most important and essential functions of states,[17] and the way in which the public schools are financed is central to performance of the function. Consequently, the Court would probably not interpret the Constitution as permitting Congress to require states to implement a tuition system.

Thus, Congress could develop a tuition system in the public schools by attaching conditions to the funds it provides to states for education but not by legislative mandate. Given the magnitude of federal spending for education, a tuition system would probably be adopted widely if it were a prerequisite for federal funds. At the same time, the undoubted authority of government to require attendance at school for the period of time necessary to acquire basic skills[18] permits the system to place a financial burden on parents that will discourage childbearing.[19]

## NOTES

1. Bureau of the Census, U.S. Department of Commerce, Statistical Abstract of the United States: 1980, 101st ed., 162, 440 (Washington, D.C.: U.S. Gov't. Printing Office, 1980); Bureau of the Census, U.S. Department of Commerce, Historical Statistics of the United States: Colonial Times to 1970 373 (Washington, D.C.: U.S. Gov't. Printing Office, 1975).
2. 411 U.S. 1 (1973).
3. *Id.* at 25 n.60.
4. Brown v Bd. of Educ., 347 U.S. 483, 493 (1954).
5. Kruse v Campbell, 431 F.Supp. 180, 184 n.4, 186–89 (E.D. Va. 1977) (three judge court), *vacated with directions to decide case on statutory grounds,* 434 U.S. 808 (1977).
6. Zablocki v Redhail, 434 U.S. 374, 387 (1978).
7. 411 U.S. at 35.
8. Guadalupe Organization, Inc. v Tempe Elementary School Dist., 587 F.2d 1022 (9th Cir. 1978).
9. Lau v Nichols, 483 F.2d 791 (9th Cir. 1973), *reversed on statutory grounds,* 414 U.S. 563 (1974).
10. *Id.* at 797. *See* Martin Luther King Jr. Elementary School Children v Michigan Bd. of Educ., 451 F.Supp. 1324 (E.D. Mich. 1978).
11. Dandridge v Williams, 397 U.S. 471 (1970).
12. *Id.* at 486; Maher v Roe, 432 U.S. 464 (1977).
13. Cleland v Nat'l College of Business, 435 U.S. 213, 221 n.9 (1978).
14. Bureau of the Census, U.S. Department of Commerce, Statistical Abstract of the United States: 1980, 101st ed., 161 (Washington, D.C.: U.S. Gov't. Printing Office, 1980).
15. Lau v Nichols, 414 U.S. 563, 569 (1974); King v Smith, 392 U.S. 309, 333 n.34 (1968).
16. Nat'l League of Cities v Usery, 426 U.S. 833, 851 (1976).
17. Wisconsin v Yoder, 406 U.S. 205, 213 (1972); Ambach v Norwick, 441 U.S. 68, 76 (1979).
18. "There is no doubt as to the power of a State, having a high responsibility for education of its citizens, to impose reasonable regulations for the control and duration of basic education." Wisconsin v Yoder, 406 U.S. 205, 213 (1972).
19. Parents have the option of sending their children to private schools; the Constitution prohibits the government from compelling children to attend public schools. Pierce v Society of Sisters, 268 U.S. 510 (1925). A child sent to a private school will face a tuition charge at least as high as that imposed in public schools.

# IV TWO CONTEMPORARY CONTROVERSIAL ISSUES

# 10 ABORTION

The current era of constitutional law relevant to abortion began on January 22, 1973, when the Supreme Court announced its decision in *Roe v Wade*. The Court's opinion placed severe limitations on government action restricting access to abortion.[1] The incidence of abortion has risen rapidly as the result of *Roe*. The number of legal abortions was estimated to be 745,000 in 1973 and 1,410,000 in 1978; the proportion of women in their reproductive years undergoing an abortion rose from 1.7 percent in 1973 to 2.8 percent in 1978.[2] At the same time that abortion has become more frequent, it has become an important political issue; in 1980, the Republican party adopted a platform calling for a constitutional amendment that would overturn the *Roe* decision and prohibit abortion.[3]

At issue in *Roe v Wade* was a state statute, typical of those in force in the United States, that imposed criminal penalties on anyone performing or attempting to perform an abortion unless the procedure was necessary to save the life of the pregnant woman. The Court began its opinion by noting that statutes regulating abortion generally appeared only in the last half of the nineteenth century; the common law had been in effect in most states until that time.

Under common law, abortion was not a criminal offense prior to recognizable movement of the fetus in the uterus, which usually occurs in the fourth month of pregnancy, and was probably not an offense after fetal movement had been detected. In the nineteenth century the common law was superseded by restrictive statutes because of the hazards abortion posed to women's health and a concern with the life, or potential life, of the fetus.

## RIGHT OF PRIVACY

In evaluating the validity of the statutes regulating abortion, the Court utilized the right of privacy that it had inferred from the guarantee of liberty in the due process clauses of the Constitution.[4] No right of privacy appears explicitly in the Constitution, but the Court viewed the assurance that no person will be deprived of "liberty without due process of law" as providing a basis for protecting a wide variety of matters concerning family life, including decisions whether to have a child. The right of privacy, however, was not held to be absolute; the Court ruled that, given sufficiently important objectives and carefully tailored means, government could curtail exercise of the right. Two compelling government interests were found to outweigh the right of privacy, protection of the health of the woman and protection of the potential life of the fetus. The Court viewed the matter as follows:

> The pregnant woman cannot be isolated in her privacy. She carries an embryo and, later, a fetus, if one accepts the medical definitions of the developing young in the human uterus. The situation therefore is inherently different from [previous cases dealing with marriage, contraception, and childrearing. It] is reasonable and appropriate for a State to decide that at some point in time another interest, that of health of the mother or that of potential human life, becomes significantly involved. The woman's privacy is no longer sole and any right of privacy she possesses must be measured accordingly.[5]

The Court held that the state's interest in the health of the pregnant woman becomes compelling and outweighs her constitutional right of privacy when the probability of death from abortion matches the probability of death from carrying the pregnancy to term. On the basis of existing medical knowledge, the point was placed at approximately the end of the first trimester of pregnancy.[6] The Court held that the state's interest in the potential life of the fetus did not become compelling at conception; the unborn are not "persons" within the meaning of the due process clauses. Rather, the state's interest in potential human life becomes compelling at the time the fetus is capable of living outside the uterus, even though life must be sustained by artificial life support systems. Given current medical technology, this point occurs at roughly the start of the third trimester of pregnancy.

As each of the two interests becomes compelling, the extent of permissible government regulation of abortion increases. In the period when no compelling interest exists—roughly the first trimester of pregnancy—decisions regarding abortion are to be made solely by women and their physicians, and no governmental interference is possible. In the period when there are legitimate grounds for concern about the impact of abortion on the health of the pregnant woman—a period which begins approximately at the start of the second trimester—government may impose reasonable regulations designed to protect women's health. In the period when a compelling interest exists in protecting the viable fetus—roughly during the third trimester—government may prohibit abortions unless they are necessary to preserve women's physical or mental health.[7] Government regulation of abortion, in short, can increase as the pregnancy continues and the fetus develops, but only in the final phase is government permitted to prohibit the procedure—and then not under all conditions. In the words of the Court:

> This holding, we feel, is consistent with the relative weights of the respective interests involved, with the lessons and examples of medical and legal history, with the lenity of the common law, and with the demands of the profound problems of the present day. The decision leaves the State free to place increasing restrictions on abortion as the period of pregnancy lengthens, so long as those restrictions are tailored to the recognized state interests. The decision vindicates the right of the physician to administer medical treatment according to his professional judgment up to the points where important state interests provide compelling justifications for intervention. Up to those points, the abortion decision in all its aspects is inherently, and primarily, a medical decision, and basic responsibility for it must rest with the physician.[8]

## RESPONSIBILITY OF PHYSICIANS

The principle that the individual physician bears the responsibility for decisions whether to perform an abortion on a pregnant woman — and, by implication, for the conduct of the procedure — appears in a number of situations. The Supreme Court has held that government cannot require first-trimester abortions to be performed in hospitals because there is no evidence that the procedure is more hazardous when done in freestanding clinics. The Court has also held that, once the attending physician has decided the procedure is desirable, government cannot require that other physicians concur in the judgment or that abortions performed in hospitals be approved in advance by a committee.[9] In addition, a statutory prohibition on the use of saline amniocentesis to induce abortions after the first trimester has been invalidated; the technique was the one most commonly employed by physicians and was safer from the perspective of maternal mortality than was carrying the pregnancy to term. The Court has also struck down a statute that required a physician performing an abortion to utilize the same level of professional skill to preserve the life and health of an aborted fetus that he or she would utilize to preserve the life and health of a fetus that was not to be aborted. The Court concluded that the statute imposed on the physician a duty that was unacceptable prior to viability of the fetus.[10]

Even after the fetus is deemed viable, the Court has ruled, a statute with criminal sanctions cannot be used to require the attending physician to choose the abortion technique that yields the highest probability of fetus survival unless another technique is necessary to protect the life and health of the pregnant woman. Statutes imposing criminal penalties must not be ambiguous but must provide a person of average intelligence with reasonable notice that particular conduct is prohibited. Uncertainty in respect to abortion, the Court found, was unavoidable because selection of the most appropriate technique for performing an abortion is complex and necessitates medical judgment involving criteria on which physicians are not always in agreement. Moreover, the statute in question did not clearly provide that the interests of the woman must always prevail over those of the fetus, especially since there was no specification of the factors to be considered by a physician in judging the health of the pregnant woman. The Court concluded as follows:

> Consequently, it is uncertain whether the statute permits the physician to consider his duty to the patient to be paramount to his duty to the fetus, or whether it requires the physician to make a "trade-off" between the woman's health and additional percentage points of fetal survival. Serious ethical and constitutional difficulties, that we do not address, lurk behind this ambiguity. We hold only that where conflicting duties of this magnitude are involved, the State, at the least, must proceed with greater precision before it may subject a physician to possible criminal sanctions.[11]

## VIABILITY OF THE FETUS

With regard to the issue of fetal viability, the Court has stated that a fetus is to be deemed viable when the attending physician, after considering all relevant factors, finds a reasonable probability that the fetus can survive outside the uterus, with or without assistance from medical technology and equipment. Because multiple criteria are involved in this determination and because viability can be reached at different times in the gestation process, a statute cannot take the decision out of the hands of the physician or establish one standard for viability—for example, a certain number of weeks of gestation or a certain fetal weight.[12] Determinations regarding viability—and every other medical aspect of the abortion procedure—fall within the purview of the duly licensed physician.

Physician control over abortion, it should be stressed, extends only to the medical aspects of the procedure. Prior to the procedure, the informed written consent of the pregnant woman can constitutionally be required. Written consent to abortion, the Court ruled, can be mandated at any stage of pregnancy, because the patient has an obvious interest in the surgery to which she will be subjected:

> The decision to abort, indeed, is an important and often a stressful one, and it is desirable and imperative that it be made with full knowledge of its nature and consequences. The woman is the one primarily concerned, and her awareness of the decision and its significance may be assured, constitutionally, by the State to the extent of requiring her prior written consent.[13]

However, other than that consent be in written form, the conditions necessary for the existence of informed consent have generally been viewed as not a constititionally proper subject for government determination. For example, lower federal courts have invalidated statutes directing that women be advised of the possible medical and psychological consequences of abortion, pregnancy, and childbirth.[14] At the same time, most courts that have considered mandatory twenty-four- or forty-eight-hour waiting periods between the initial medical consultation and the abortion procedure have invalidated them; the courts viewed whatever benefit such waiting periods might provide as offset by the consequent reduction in the safety and accessibility of the abortion procedure.[15] The judiciary has also struck down legislation requiring the attending physician to advise women, in terms calculated to produce an emotional response, of the anatomical and physiological characteristics of the fetus. Such a requirement was viewed as interfering in the physician-patient relationship and as preventing physicians from deciding how best to treat their patients, some of whom would not be well served by receiving the information.[16] The type and extent of knowledge a woman needs in order to give informed consent to an abortion, in short, is to be determined by her physician.

## CONSENT OF OTHER PERSONS

The question has arisen in constitutional litigation whether the consent of persons other than the pregnant woman can be required before an abortion is performed. The question involves two classes of persons: the woman's spouse and, in the case of a minor, her parents.

### Spousal Consent

The Supreme Court has invalidated a statute that required the written consent of the spouse of a married woman for a first-trimester abortion unless the abortion was necessary to preserve the life of the woman. The principal ground for the Court's decision was that government cannot delegate the power to deny a first-trimester abortion when it does not itself have the power of denial. Moreover, the Court concluded that, in the event of a disagreement between a husband and a wife on the issue of whether the wife should have an abortion, the interest of the wife must prevail because she is more affected by the pregnancy:

> [T]he marital couple is not an independent entity with a mind and heart of its own, but an association of two individuals, each with a separate intellectual and emotional makeup. If the right of privacy means anything, it is the right of the *individual,* married or single, to be free from unwarranted governmental intrusion into matters so fundamentally affecting a person as the decision whether to bear or beget a child. ...
>
> [The statute requiring spousal consent] "does much more than insure that the husband participate in the decision whether his wife should have an abortion. The State, instead, has determined that the husband's interest in continuing the pregnancy of his wife always outweighs any interest on her part in terminating it irrespective of the condition of their marriage. The State, accordingly, has granted him the right to prevent unilaterally, and for whatever reason, the effectuation of his wife's and her physician's decision to terminate her pregnancy. This state determination ... has interposed an absolute obstacle to a woman's decision that *Roe [v Wade]* held to be constitutionally protected from such interference.[17]

The opinion leaves a number of questions unanswered. First, can the consent of the husband be required for abortions in the second and third trimester? Second, even if his consent is not needed in any trimester, can government mandate that a husband be notified that his wife is seeking an abortion? With regard to the first question, one lower federal court has held that spousal consent cannot be required for second-trimester abortions because, under *Roe v Wade,* government cannot prohibit abortions at this stage but can act only to promote the health of the woman.[18] Regardless of the judiciary's position on this question, however, only 9 percent of all abortions are performed after the first trimester;[19] therefore, the issue of spousal consent will affect relatively few abortions. With regard to the second question, another court has ruled that a statute mandating notice to the spouse is unconstitutional when it fails to permit exceptions for circumstances where notice may not be desirable — for instance, where the husband is not the father of the fetus, where the wife is the victim of rape, or where the husband is mentally ill.[20] Having been rendered by lower courts, these decisions do not provide definitive answers to the role of the husband in abortion, but they are the best evidence to date of the direction the law will take.

## Parental Consent

As troublesome as the interest of the husband is the weight to be accorded the interest of the parents whose minor unmarried daughter is pregnant and wants an abortion. The number of such parents is appreciable. Research has estimated that in 1976, 14.4 percent of all females had experienced a premarital pregnancy before reaching age eighteen, an increase of 2.5 percentage points over the level of 1971;[21] at the same time, the proportion of females under eighteen years of age who bear children has declined since the early 1970s[22] because of the greater utilization of abortion.[23] What role can parents constitutionally play in the decision of their minor daughters to have an abortion? The Supreme Court has accepted the principle that, because minors lack sufficient experience, government can regulate their conduct more extensively than it can regulate the conduct of adults. The state has the authority to protect minors from themselves and to promote the ability of parents to direct and rear their children. Accordingly, prohibitions backed by criminal sanctions can be imposed on the sale of erotic materials to minors, even though the materials are not obscene and their sale to adults cannot be blocked.[24] However, minors do not totally lack constitutional protections. The ability of government to control minors does indeed encounter constitutional restraints, but controls can be more rigorous for them than for adults without implicating such restraints.

With regard to abortion, the conditions under which government can authorize parents to intervene and the extent of the permitted intervention are not completely clear. Two sets of distinctions need to be made—first, between a requirement of parental consent and a requirement of parental notification; and second, between mature minors and immature minors. A minor capable of understanding the implications of abortion—that is, a mature minor—cannot be required to obtain parental consent in order to have an abortion, but there is no definitive answer from the Court regarding whether a requirement for parental notification prior to abortion is constitutionally valid for such a minor. A minor who is psychologically immature and dependent on her parents may be denied access to an abortion until her parents are notified, if such notification is possible.[25] An immature minor can apparently be required to secure the consent of her parents in order to undergo an abortion; the Court has stated that not "every minor, regardless of age or maturity, may give effective consent for termination of her pregnancy."[26] However, parental consent cannot be an absolute barrier to an abortion for an immature minor when important reasons create a need for an abortion; the Court has concluded that "a state may not constitutionally legislate a blanket, unreviewable power of parents to veto their daughter's abortion."[27] Unfortunately, the Court has not had occasion to specify the reasons that would require government to provide an immature minor with access to an abortion.[28]

## GOVERNMENT FUNDING OF ABORTION FOR INDIGENT WOMEN

Government funding of abortions for indigent women has been the subject of considerable political controversy. The Supreme Court has rendered two decisions on whether such funding is mandated by the Constitution. In the first, a state regulation allowed public funds to be used to cover the expenses of childbirth and medically necessary abortions but not the expenses of medically unnecessary abortions.[29] The Court began by pointing out that the Constitution does not require government to supply funds for medical expenses incurred by indigents but that, when government does so, constitutional criteria must be satisfied. The regulation in question involved both the wealth of individuals and access to abortions. Wealth differences implicated the restrictions on classifications imposed by the equal protection clause, and the refusal to provide public funds for medically unnecessary abortions implicated the right of privacy emanating from the due process clause.[30] In deciding upon the constitutional standard to be employed to test the regulation, the Court concluded that the reasonable basis test should be used. There was no finding of a suspect classification by wealth or a serious infringement on the fundamental right of privacy—either of which would have necessitated use of the compelling interest test—because indigent women were not precluded from securing an abortion by any action on the part of government. The state regulation did not impose on indigent women any burdens that did not already exist; the state was not responsible for their poverty and did not create an obstacle of any kind to obtaining an abortion. Since a reasonable basis existed in the state's interest in encouraging childbirth, the Court upheld the regulation:

> Our conclusion signals no retreat from *Roe [v Wade]* or the cases applying it. There is a basic difference between direct state interference with a protected activity and state encouragement of an alternative activity consonant with legislative policy. Constitutional concerns are greatest when the State attempts to impose its will by force of law; the State's power to encourage actions deemed to be in the public interest is necessarily far broader.[31]

This line of reasoning was applied in a second case to a federal statute that prohibited the use of public funds for even medically necessary abortions unless the abortions were required to terminate life-threatening pregnancies.[32] *Roe v Wade* had held that, because the right of privacy would be severely infringed, abortions could not be forbidden at any stage of pregnancy when they were essential to protect the health of pregnant women, but no serious infringement on the right of privacy was found here because government had done nothing that contributed to the difficulties indigent women faced in securing abortions. As long as government had a reasonable basis for its decision—and such a basis could be found in the encouragement of childbirth—the Court saw no constitutional obligation to provide public funds for abortions when pregnancy threatened the health of indigent women. The Court concluded:

> [A]lthough government may not place obstacles in the path of a woman's exercise of her freedom of choice, it need not remove those not of its own creation. Indigency falls in the latter category. The financial constraints that restrict an indigent woman's ability to enjoy the full range of constitutionally protected freedom of choice are the product not of governmental restrictions on access to abortions, but rather of her indigency. Although

Congress has opted to subsidize medically necessary services generally, but not certain medically necessary abortions, the fact remains that the [present statute] leaves an indigent woman with at least the same range of choice in deciding whether to obtain a medically necessary abortion as she would have had if Congress had chosen to subsidize no health care costs at all.[33]

While the issue of government funding has attracted considerable attention, it appears that the availability of public monies is generally not a critical factor in the ability of indigent women to procure abortions. There is evidence that four out of five women who would have had an abortion with public funds will succeed in terminating their pregnancies without such funds[34] and that the single most important factor in the use of abortion is the extent to which abortion services are present in a community.[35] Since about two-thirds of all abortions are performed in freestanding clinics,[36] the existence of clinics specializing in abortions is particularly important to the frequency with which the procedure is employed. Attempts have been made by state and local governments to regulate, and thus restrict, abortion clinics, but the four U.S. Courts of Appeals that have considered regulations imposed on clinics performing first-trimester abortions have concluded that the regulations are constitutionally valid only if they are applicable to clinics providing all types of health services. Clinics for first-trimester abortions, and the abortion procedure itself, cannot be singled out for special regulations.[37]

In conclusion, government need not act affirmatively to extend abortion services to its citizens, but it cannot restrict access to the services except in limited ways and circumstances. The limitations on government can be summarized by five principles. First, abortion must remain free from any regulation not designed to cover medical procedures generally until the point at which the probability of death from abortion reaches the probability of death from carrying the pregnancy to term (a point that occurs roughly at the start of the second trimester of pregnancy). Second, until this point the decision whether and where to have an abortion is the concern of the woman and her physician, and no third party can intervene in the decision-making process unless the woman is an unmarried minor who lacks the maturity to understand the implications of abortion, in which case the parents have an as yet undefined role to play. Third, after the point when the risk of death from abortion equals the risk of death from childbirth, government can impose regulations on the abortion procedure that are reasonably likely to protect the health of the woman. Fourth, a prohibition on abortion is permissible only after the fetus becomes viable—a condition that is to be determined solely by the attending physician and that normally occurs roughly at the start of the third trimester. Even at this point a prohibition is not possible when the physical or mental health of the women is jeopardized. Fifth, within the limits created by the interests of government in the health of the pregnant woman and in the potential life of the viable fetus, abortion and its essential elements are completely under the control of the attending physician. The termination of pregnancy is a medical procedure, and after legitimate government interests are satisfied, the Constitution demands that the physician be protected from interference.

## NOTES

1. Roe v Wade, 410 U.S. 113 (1973).
2. Stanley Henshaw, Jacqueline Forrest, Ellen Sullivan, & Christopher Tietze, *Abortion in the United States, 1978-1979*, 13 Family Planning Perspectives 6, 7 (1981).

Of all abortions, the proportion performed on women who had previously had an abortion was estimated to be 15 percent in 1974 and 23 percent in 1976. Christopher Tietze, *Repeat Abortions—Why More?* 10 Family Planning Perspectives 286 (1978). *See generally* Patricia Steinhoff, Roy Smith, J. Palmore, M. Diamond, & C. Chung, *Women Who Obtain Repeat Abortions: A Study Based on Record Linkage*, 11 Family Planning Perspectives 30 (1979).

3. The platform provides as follows:

> There can be no doubt that the question of abortion, despite the complex nature of its various issues, is ultimately concerned with equality of rights under the law. While we recognize differing views on this question among Americans in general—and in our own party—we affirm our support of a constitutional amendment to restore protection of the right to life for unborn children. We also support the Congressional efforts to restrict the use of taxpayers' dollars for abortion.

National Abortion Rights Action League, 12 Newsletter 6 (August, 1980).

4. *Roe v Wade* utilized the due process clause of the Fourteenth Amend-

ment, which is applicable to the action of States, because the statute in dispute was that of a State. The due process clause of the Fifth Amendment, however, provides identical protections from action of the federal government. See Harris v McRae, 100 S.Ct. 2671, 2685 (1980).

5. Roe v Wade, *supra* note 1, at 159.
6. Recent evidence indicates that abortion is safer than childbirth until the sixteenth week (i.e., the fourth month) of pregnancy. Willard Cates & Christopher Tietze, *Standardized Mortality Rates Associated with Legal Abortion: United States, 1972-1975*, 10 Family Planning Perspectives 109 (1978).
7. *Roe v Wade* states that abortion cannot be forbidden after fetal viability if the "life or health" of the woman is jeopardized. No definition is given for the term *health*. However, two years earlier, a statute had been considered that prohibited abortions except when they were required to preserve the "life or health" of the pregnant woman; the Court rejected the argument that the term *health* was ambiguous and defined it to include both mental and physical well-being. United States v Vuitch, 402 U.S. 62, 72 (1971). In using the term *health* in *Roe v Wade*, the Court evidently adopted the same definition. Indeed, the Court cited its earlier decision in referring to the question of whether the statute before it was vague. 410 U.S. at 164.
8. Roe v Wade, 410 U.S. at 165-66.
9. Doe v Bolton, 410 U.S. 179 (1973).
10. Planned Parenthood of Central Missouri v Danforth, 428 U.S. 52 (1976).
11. Colautti v Franklin, 439 U.S. 379, 400-401 (1979).
12. *Id.* at 388-89; Planned Parenthood of Central Missouri v Danforth, *supra* note 10, at 64.
13. Planned Parenthood of Central Missouri v Danforth, *supra* note 10, at 67.
14. Women's Services, P.C. v Thone, 636 F.2d 206 (8th Cir. 1980); Margaret S. v Edwards, 488 F.Supp. 181 (E.D. La. 1980); Leigh v Olson, 497 F.Supp. 1340 (D. N.D. 1980).
15. *Compare* Charles v Carey, 627 F.2d 772 (7th Cir. 1980) *and* Women's Services, P.C. v Thone, *supra* note 14, *with* Wolfe v Schroering, 541 F.2d 523 (6th Cir. 1976). See generally Michael Lupfer & Bohne Silber, *How Patients View Mandatory Waiting Periods for Abortion*, 13 Family Planning Perspectives 75 (1981).
16. Charles v Carey, *supra* note 15; Planned Parenthood Ass'n v Ashcroft, 483 F.Supp. 679 (W.D. Mo. 1980); Akron Center for Reproductive Health, Inc. v City of Akron, 479 F.Supp. 1172 (N.D. Ohio 1979); Margaret S. v Edwards, *supra* note 14. See Planned Parenthood v Bellotti, 499 F.Supp. 215 (D. Mass. 1980).
17. Planned Parenthood of Central Missouri v Danforth, *supra* note 10, at 70 n.11.
18. Wolfe v Schroering, *supra* note 15.
19. Henshaw, Forrest, Sullivan, & Tietze, *supra* note 2, at 17.
20. Scheinberg v Smith, 482 F.Supp. 529 (S.D. Fla. 1979).

21. Melvin Zelnik, Young Kim, & John Kantner, *Probabilities of Intercourse and Conception among U.S. Teenage Women, 1971 and 1976*, 11 Family Planning Perspectives 177, 183 (1979).

22. National Center for Health Statistics, U.S. Department of Health & Human Services, *Final Natality Statistics, 1978*, Monthly Vital Statistics Report, vol. 29, no. 1 Supp. [DHHS Pub. No. (PHS) 80-1120] (1980), at 12; National Center for Health Statistics, U.S. Department of Health, Education & Welfare, *Teenage Childbearing: United States, 1966-75*, Monthly Vital Statistics Report, vol. 26, no. 5 Supp. [DHEW Pub. No. (HRA) 77-1120] (1977), at 9.

23. Melvin Zelnik & John Kantner, *First Pregnancies to Women Aged 15-19: 1976 and 1971*, 10 Family Planning Perspectives 11, 13, 14 (1978).

24. Ginsburg v New York, 390 U.S. 629 (1968).

25. H.L. v Matheson, 101 S.Ct. 1164 (1981).

26. Planned Parenthood of Central Missouri v Danforth, *supra* note 10, at 75.

27. H.L. v Matheson, *supra* note 25, at 1171.

28. As to the procedures by which parental denial of consent may be overruled, see Bellotti v Baird, 443 U.S. 622 (1979).

29. Maher v Roe, 432 U.S. 464 (1977).

30. The equal protection clause of the Fourteenth Amendment provides that "[n]o State shall . . . deny to any person within its jurisdiction the equal protection of the laws." A guarantee of equal protection applicable to the federal government has been inferred from the due process clause of the Fifth Amendment. Hampton v Wong, 426 U.S. 88 (1976). See note 4, *supra*.

31. Maher v Roe, 432 U.S. at 475-76.

32. Harris v McRae, 448 U.S. 297 (1980).

33. *Id.* at 316-317.

34. James Trussell, Jane Menken, Barbara Lindheim, & Barbara Vaughan, *The Impact of Restricting Medicaid Financing for Abortion*, 12 Family Planning Perspectives 120 (1980).

35. Jeff Borders & Phillips Cutright, *Community Determinants of U.S. Legal Abortion Rates*, 11 Family Planning Perspectives 227 (1979).

36. Jacqueline Forrest, Ellen Sullivan, & Christopher Tietze, *Abortion in the United States, 1977-1978*, 11 Family Planning Perspectives 329, 335 (1979).

37. Baird v Dep't of Pub. Health, 599 F.2d 1098 (1st Cir. 1979); Friendship Medical Center, Ltd. v Chicago Bd. of Health, 505 F.2d 1141 (7th Cir. 1974), *cert. denied*, 420 U.S. 997 (1975); Hodgson v Lawson, 542 F.2d 1350 (8th Cir. 1976); Mahoning Women's Center v Hunter, 610 F.2d 456 (6th Cir. 1979), *vacated and remanded on other grounds*, 100 S.Ct. 3006 (1980).

# 11 IMMIGRATION

The immigration of aliens into the United States has historically been an important factor in the growth of the country's population.[1] Unfortunately, the demographic aspects of current immigration and its future impact have not been well studied. Indeed, demographic research presently is capable only of making estimates of unknown accuracy with regard to the volume and characteristics of immigrants, particularly those who enter the country illegally.[2] However, while research on immigration is scanty, a substantial body of constitutional law exists on the subject. Our concern is to examine the constitutional authority of Congress to restrict immigration as a means of controlling population size and the authority of government at all levels to treat aliens already within the United States differently from citizens in order to discourage further immigration.

## CONGRESSIONAL AUTHORITY OVER IMMIGRATION

The authority of Congress to regulate immigration does not appear to emanate from a single provision of the Constitution. Article I,

Section 8 delegates to Congress the power "to establish a uniform rule of naturalization," but federal authority over immigration apparently rests on a broader foundation. The Supreme Court has indicated on several occasions that the authority arises from the sovereignty of the United States as a nation.[3] Immigration is under the control of Congress simply because Congress is the repository of legislative authority for an independent nation in a world of nations. Since the regulation of immigration is an aspect of the external affairs of the United States, the admission of aliens is normally a question that is outside the scope of the Constitution.[4] Accordingly, Congress can prohibit all immigration if it chooses to do so.[5] When a certain numerical level of immigration is allowed, the types of persons permitted entry into the country are totally within the discretion of Congress.[6]

If control over the admission of aliens is not a complicated constitutional issue, the regulation of aliens already within the United States is. To the extent that government can restrict economic opportunities for resident aliens, immigration can be expected to fall.[7]

### Aliens in Public Employment

Most of the Supreme Court cases relevant to economic opportunities for aliens have concerned limitations imposed on employment. With regard to public employment, the Court has invalidated a state statute that excluded all aliens from permanent positions in the state civil service system.[8] The Court held that the statute violated the equal protection clause of the Fourteenth Amendment, which provides that a state cannot "deny to any person within its jurisdiction the equal protection of the laws" through the use of unjustifiable classifications. The clause protects persons, not just citizens, and is hence applicable to aliens. The Court had earlier held that classifications based on the fact of alien status were "suspect" under the clause and that such classifications were constitutionally valid only if they served a compelling government interest and were narrowly drawn so as to further only that interest.[9] The statute prohibiting aliens from holding permanent positions in the state civil service system was found to be invalid because it was not narrowly drawn. A state has a legitimate interest in promoting the values and ideals of the community it governs, but the statute excluded aliens from positions that had no bearing on the interest; under the statute, for example, an alien could not be employed as a garbage collector or a typist. The strict scrutiny test, the Court concluded, demanded greater precision.

The Court has, however, created an exception to the use of the compelling interest standard for classifications involving aliens. The Court has held that the classifications need only possess a reasonable basis when they are applied to employment in integral governmental functions. Rather than continue the use of the strict test and hold that the performance of governmental functions constitutes a compelling interest, the Court has chosen to adopt the reasonable basis standard for classifications limiting the employment of aliens where governmental functions are performed:

> The rule for governmental functions, which is an exception to the general standard applicable to classifications based on alienage, rests on important principles inherent in the Constitution. The distinction between citizens and aliens, though ordinarily irrelevant to private activity, is fundamental to the definition and government of a State. The Constitution itself refers to the distinction no less than 11 times, indicating that the status of citizenship was meant to have significance in the structure of our government. The assumption of that status, whether by birth or naturalization, denotes an association with the polity which, in a democratic republic, exercises the power of governance. The form of this association is important: an oath of allegiance or similar ceremony cannot substitute for the unequivocal legal bond citizenship represents. It is because of this special significance of citizenship that governmental entities, when exercising the functions of government, have wider latitude in limiting the participation of noncitizens.[10]

Accordingly, the Court has upheld a state statute prohibiting aliens eligible for citizenship from serving as public school teachers if they did not intend to become citizens.[11] Because schools teach children about the nature and values of the American political system and the duties of citizenship, the Court concluded that public education constituted a governmental function. A reasonable basis for the statute was found in the fact that only aliens who voluntarily chose not to become citizens were excluded from teaching positions in the public schools; these aliens could reasonably be assumed to possess less sympathy toward, and a lesser understanding of, American traditions and institutions.

The Court has also concluded that a state statute prohibiting aliens from serving as police officers is constitutional[12] because police protection is a governmental function; police officers execute official public policy in enforcing the law. A reasonable basis for excluding aliens from the police force was found in the significant judgment and discretion required of police; citizens can reasonably be assumed to have more acquaintance with, and sympathy for, American traditions and values that affect the manner in which laws are enforced.

The exclusion of aliens from public employment, then, is subject to the reasonable basis test if the employment concerns the performance of governmental functions, but to the compelling interest test if the employment concerns the performance of nongovernmental functions.

### Aliens in Private Employment

Only future litigation will fully define the range of governmental functions, but it seems clear at this point that private employment bears closer similarities to nongovernmental functions. Accordingly, statutes and regulations that exclude aliens from private employment can be expected to encounter a strict standard of review that makes such exclusions constitutionally doubtful.

In 1915 the Supreme Court considered a state statute that prohibited private employers of five or more employees from filling more than 20 percent of the positions with aliens.[13] The Court held that the statute violated the equal protection clause because no legitimate state interest was served by limiting the right to employment of aliens who had been lawfully admitted into the United States. Not only did aliens have a Fourteenth Amendment right to pursue employment free from unnecessary restrictions, but the federal government had permitted the aliens subject to the statute to enter this country, and the states could not frustrate the federal power over immigration by denying or reducing the employment

# IMMIGRATION

opportunities of persons who had been properly admitted. The Court concluded:

> It is sought to justify this act as an exercise of the power of the State to make reasonable classifications in legislating to promote the health, safety, morals and welfare of those within its jurisdiction. But this admitted authority, with the broad range of legislative discretion that it implies, does not go so far as to make it possible for the State to deny to lawful inhabitants, because of their race or nationality, the ordinary means of earning a livelihood. It requires no argument to show that the right to work for a living in the common occupations of the community is of the very essence of the personal freedom and opportunity that it was the purpose of the [Fourteenth] Amendment to secure. If this could be refused solely upon the ground of race or nationality, the prohibition of the denial to any person of the equal protection of the laws would be a barren form of words. It is no answer to say, as it is argued, that the act proceeds upon the assumption that "the employment of aliens unless restrained was a peril to the public welfare." The discrimination against aliens in the wide range of employments to which the act relates is made an end in itself and thus the authority to deny to aliens, upon the mere fact of their alienage, the right to obtain support in the ordinary fields of labor is necessarily involved. It must also be said that reasonable classification implies action consistent with the legitimate interests of the State, and it will not be disputed that these cannot be so broadly conceived as to bring them into hostility to exclusive Federal power. The authority to control immigration—to admit or exclude aliens—is vested solely in the Federal Government. The assertion of an authority to deny to aliens the opportunity of earning a livelihood when lawfully admitted to the State would be tantamount to the assertion of the right to deny them entrance and abode, for in ordinary cases they cannot live where they cannot work. And, if such a policy were permissible, the practical result would be that those lawfully admitted to the country under the authority of the acts of Congress, instead of enjoying in a substantial sense and in their full scope the privileges conferred by the admission, would be segregated in such of the States as chose to offer hospitality.[14]

The Court's reasoning in the 1915 case differed from that which it would use today, but the result would be the same. In 1915 the concepts of a suspect classification and the compelling interest test had not been developed, nor did they exist in 1948 when the Court invalidated a state statute that prohibited aliens who were not eligible for citizenship from receiving commercial fishing licenses.[15]

By the early 1970s, however, the Court had developed the concepts and applied them to aliens. For example, in one case involving private employment, a state regulation that excluded aliens from obtaining a license to practice law was held to violate the equal protection clause.[16] Because a classification by alien status was constitutionally suspect, the state was required to demonstrate that its regulation advanced a compelling interest and was designed to further only that interest. Assuring that individuals possess the necessary personal and professional qualifications to practice law was held to be an important and legitimate governmental interest, but the Court found the regulation unconstitutional because it was not necessary to advance the interest. The Court reasoned that the state had the ability and authority to judge the qualifications of individuals both before their admission to the bar and during their tenure as lawyers; consequently, the total exclusion of aliens from the practice of law was an unnecessarily broad means to promote the state interest in the qualifications of lawyers.

In a second case the Court used the compelling interest test to invalidate a statute under which a civil engineer's license could be issued only to citizens.[17] In addition to the statute's interference with federal power over immigration, the Court gave two grounds for its decision. First, while issuance of a license was a way to assure that a civil engineer was financially accountable in the event of faulty workmanship, the Court found that other means were readily available to ensure accountability. The statute was thus unnecessarily broad in denying a license to aliens as a class. Second, in response to the argument that a state has a legitimate and important interest in raising the standard of living of its citizens, the Court stated that the state interest cannot be advanced by excluding lawfully admitted aliens from occupational opportunities: "To uphold the statute on the basis of broad economic justification of this kind would permit any State to bar the employment of aliens in any or all lawful occupations."[18] The advancement of economic welfare, the Court held, required more direct means.

To recapitulate, statutes and regulations that exclude aliens from employment invoke the compelling interest standard when the employer is a private firm or when the employer is the government and the position involves a nongovernmental function. When government is the employer and the position entails the performance of a governmental function, restrictive statutes are measured against the reasonable basis standard, which provides considerably greater latitude in the exclusion of aliens.

## Regulation of Public Benefits

Employment is not the only form of economic opportunity to which access has been restricted for aliens. The Supreme Court has invoked the equal protection clause when statutes and regulations have excluded aliens from public financial benefits. Two cases have been decided by the Court that involved restrictions by a state. In the first a statute denied aliens welfare assistance that was available to citizens.[19] The Court found the statute unconstitutional on the ground that, since a classification by alienage is suspect and the compelling interest standard is to be applied, the state interest in minimizing expenditures could not serve as a sufficient justification for the denial of welfare aid to aliens. A limitation of expenditures may constitute a reasonable basis for a classification, but it is not a compelling interest, especially when the classification prohibits aliens from receiving the financial assistance for which their taxes have been paying. Moreover, the Court found the state restriction in conflict with, and thus preempted by, federal statutes that, while prohibiting the admission of aliens likely to become public burdens in the future, did not authorize any penalty for aliens who in fact became burdens after their admission. A state must bow to the superior authority of the federal government when the latter has regulated a matter committed to its determination.[20]

In the second case involving financial assistance provided by a state, aliens were precluded by statute from receiving a scholarship or loan to pursue a college degree unless they had applied for citizenship or filed a statement showing that they intended to do so.[21] Even though only a subclass of aliens was subject to the restriction — namely, those who had not applied and did not intend to apply for citizenship — the Court ruled that the compelling interest standard was the appropriate test; a constitutionally suspect class had been created under the equal protection clause inasmuch as only aliens were affected by the statute. Using the strict scrutiny test, the Court ruled that the statute was invalid on the ground that no compelling state interest existed that could justify it. An interest in encouraging citizenship was impermissible for a state because control over naturalization was the exclusive prerogative of the federal government. An interest in raising the educational level of voters was not sufficient because, even though voting was a right only of citizens, aliens could effectively contribute to the political community in other ways if they possessed maximum educational opportunities. In addition, the Court noted that "[r]esident aliens are obligated to pay their full share of the taxes that support the assistance programs. There thus is no real unfairness in allowing resident aliens an equal right to participate in programs to which they contribute on an equal basis."[22]

A final case involving public financial benefits concerned the federal government rather than a state, and it resulted in an opinion whose reasoning was significantly different from that found in the prior two decisions. The case arose from a federal statute that denied a portion of Medicare insurance coverage to aliens who had not been granted permanent resident status and who had not resided in the United States for a minimum of five years.[23] The statute was challenged under the due process clause of the Fifth Amendment, which has been held to contain a guarantee of equal protection applicable to action by the federal government.[24] The Supreme Court applied the reasonable basis standard to the statute because the regulation of aliens is within the authority of the federal government rather than of the states. The Court reasoned as follows:

> [T]he responsibility for regulating the relationship between the United States and our alien visitors has been committed to the political branches of the Federal Government. Since decisions in these matters may implicate our relations with foreign powers, and since a wide variety of classifications must be defined in the light of changing political and economic circumstances, such decisions are frequently of a character more appropriate to either the Legislature or the Executive than to the Judiciary. . . . Any rule of constitutional law that would inhibit the flexibility of the political branches of government to respond to changing world conditions should be adopted only with the greatest caution.[25]

Public financial assistance from which aliens are excluded therefore generates the compelling interest standard when there is action by a state, but the reasonable basis standard when the action of the federal government is involved. Under the reasonable basis standard, the Court found the federal statute precluding aliens from securing a part of Medicare insurance coverage constitutional on the ground that it was legitimate for Congress to confine the insurance to aliens having an affinity with the United States, and it was reasonable for Congress to assume that aliens who possessed permanent resident status and who had lived in the country for at least five years were characterized by that affinity.

## ILLEGAL ALIENS

To this point we have considered cases involving aliens who were lawfully present in the United States. Although only rough estimates exist, illegal aliens appear to number at least 2 to 3 million and to be increasing by not less than 150,000 annually.[26] Since immigration is within the domain of federal authority, public and private economic opportunities can almost certainly be foreclosed to illegal aliens by statutes enacted by Congress. On the other hand, it is not certain that a state may undertake similar action. The Supreme Court has rendered only one decision relevant to the issue.[27] The decision involved a California statute that prohibited employers from knowingly hiring illegal aliens when doing so would adversely affect citizens and aliens legally present in the country. The statute was held not to be a regulation of immigration and thus not to intrude on a subject committed to federal control, not to be expressly preempted by federal law, and not to deal with a problem outside the scope of state power. The decision, however, was a very narrow one; the Court held only that the statute was not precluded by the authority of the federal government over immigration or by existing federal laws on the subject and that it was a proper exercise of the state's power to protect the welfare of its citizens. The Court did not reach the issue of whether the statute, though otherwise a legitimate exercise of state power, violated the equal protection clause. And, of course, the Court did not decide whether statutes or regulations denying illegal aliens other types of economic opportunities were constitutional. In short, the rights of aliens unlawfully present in the United States cannot be specified at this time.[28]

In conclusion, immigration will probably become an important political issue in the years ahead. World population numbers are increasing rapidly, especially in impoverished countries, and the probable result will be both pressures to permit more legal immigration and increases in illegal immigration. At the same time the American economy and standard of living will be threatened by resource shortages and environmental deterioration. These threats are likely to generate measures designed to discourage both legal and illegal immigrants from coming to and remaining in the United States. The population problem as manifested in immigration can thus be expected to have visible constitutional ramifications in the future.

## NOTES

1. C. Gibson, *The Contribution of Immigration to the United States Population Growth: 1790-1970*, 9 International Migration Review 157 (1975).
2. Charles Keely & Ellen Kraly, *Recent Net Alien Immigration to the United States: Its Impact on Population Growth and Native Fertility*, 15 Demography 267 (1978); Charles Keely, *Counting the Uncountable: Estimates of Undocumented Aliens in the United States*, 3 Population & Development Review 473 (1977); see text accompanying notes 12-13 in chapter 1.
3. Fiallo v Bell, 430 U.S. 787, 792 (1977); Harisiades v Shaughnessy, 342 U.S. 580, 587-88 (1952); Fong Yue Ting v United States, 149 U.S. 698, 705, 711 (1893); The Chinese Exclusion Case, 130 U.S. 581, 609 (1889).
4. Hampton v Wong, 426 U.S. 88, 101 n.21 (1976); Fiallo v Bell, 430 U.S. 787, 792 (1977).
5. *See* Knauff v Shaughnessy, 338 U.S. 537, 542 (1950); Ekiu v United States, 142 U.S. 651, 659 (1892).
6. The Japanese Immigrant Case, 189 U.S. 86, 97 (1903); Fiallo v Bell, 430 U.S. 787, 796 (1977).
7. House Select Committee on Population, Legal and Illegal Immigration to the United States, 95th Cong., 2d Sess. 25 (1978).
8. Sugarman v Dougall, 413 U.S. 634 (1973).
9. Graham v Richardson, 403 U.S. 365, 371-72 (1971); see also Sugarman v Dougall, 413 U.S. at 642.

10. Ambach v Norwick, 441 U.S. 68, 75 (1979).
11. *Id.*
12. Foley v Connelie, 435 U.S. 291 (1978).
13. Truax v Raich, 239 U.S. 33 (1915).
14. *Id.* at 41–42.
15. Takahashi v Fish & Game Comm'n, 334 U.S. 410 (1948).
16. In re Griffiths, 413 U.S. 717 (1973).

The Court noted that a lawyer is neither a governmental official nor so involved in the political process as to formulate governmental policy. *Id.* at 729. Cases dealing with government functions in public employment are therefore not applicable to the practice of law.

17. Examining Bd. of Engineers, Architects, & Surveyors v Otero, 426 U.S. 572 (1976).
18. *Id.* at 605–6.
19. Graham v Richardson, 403 U.S. 365 (1971).
20. When there is a conflict between a state statute and a federal statute, the former must yield because of the supremacy clause of the Constitution. The clause provides that "[t]his Constitution, and the laws of the United States which shall be made in pursuance thereof; and all treaties made, or which shall be made, under the authority of the United States, shall be the supreme law of the land." Art. VI, cl. 2.
21. Nyquist v Mauclet, 432 U.S. 1 (1977).
22. *Id.* at 12.
23. Mathews v Diaz, 426 U.S. 67 (1976).
24. Hampton v Wong, 426 U.S. 88, 100 (1976).
25. 426 U.S. at 81.
26. J. Gregory Robinson, *Estimating the Approximate Size of the Illegal Alien Population in the United States by the Comparative Trend Analysis of Age-Specific Death Rates*, 17 Demography 159, 174–75 (1980); David M. Heer, *What is the Annual Net Flow of Undocumented Mexican Immigrants to the United States?*, 16 Demography 417 (1979).

For estimates of public expenditures on illegal aliens, see *Immigration to the United States: Hearings Before the Select Committee on Population*, 95th Cong., 2d Sess. 572 (1978), statement of Burdette Wright for the County of Los Angeles. See also Task Force on Medical Care for Illegal Aliens, "The Economic Impact of Undocumented Immigrants on Public Health Services in Orange County," reprinted in *id.*, at 615.

27. De Canas v Bica, 424 U.S. 351 (1976).
28. The Supreme Court has agreed to review a Texas statute denying free public education to the children of illegal immigrants. Doe v Plyler, 628 F.2d 448 (5th Cir. 1980), *cert. granted* –U.S.–(1981) (No. 80-1538). See also In re Alien Children Education Litigation, 501 F.Supp. 544 (S.D. Tex. 1980).

# AFTERWORD

The preceding chapters have been organized around a theme in a manner that, I hope, will make the book a useful contribution to the literature. The purpose has been to link law and demography. Unfortunately, legal scholars and demographers have lived in their separate worlds, with little discourse between them, and since only a handful of people have acquired expertise in both law and demography, the link between the two fields has been overlooked. Yet, as one observer has noted: "The subject of law and demography is a very important and often neglected area which has been hampered by the lack of personnel who have an understanding of both law and demography. Heretofore, the literature has been dominated by either lawyers writing in a classical legal tradition or by demographers writing in a classical social science tradition."[1] The book will, I hope, promote the cross-fertilization of concepts and principles from the two fields.

The theme of the book—that the United States is facing a serious problem of overpopulation and needs to adopt a formal fertility control policy—is not new.[2] Nor is it widely accepted, and it is not likely to be for some time to come. Established ideas die slowly, and only through recurring social, economic, and ecological problems that resist solution are the American people likely to realize that new solutions must be found and population numbers limited.

A fertility control policy will probably not be forthcoming until a major change occurs in Americans' perspective of the world around them.[3] The way in which we perceive and define the world must undergo a major alteration; our picture of reality must be redrawn. The philosophy that growth is desirable and inevitable must give way to the recognition that we live in a world of finite resources, that technology can stretch those resources only so far, and that ultimately we must limit the number of people in the United States if we are to avoid dividing the pie into ever-smaller pieces that require a continuing reduction in our standard of living.

The elements of a high standard of living are not divinely inspired but are personally defined, and I am aware that the theme of the book is based upon a set of assumptions about what constitutes those elements. Let me attempt to make them explicit. The central element can be identified as freedom — freedom to move physically without constant contacts with other people necessitated by life in densely populated areas and without restrictions imposed by government, which become more frequent as human numbers increase.[4] A related element is the availability of, and access to, large amounts of space for each individual. Crowded living is not pleasant. A third element is access to rewarding employment opportunities. Excessive population numbers damage employment prospects by providing a large supply of individuals for existing positions and by reducing the availability of natural resources, including energy, that permit a healthy, productive economy.[5] A fourth element is an environment uncontaminated by noxious stimuli such as toxic chemicals. As economic activity expands in an attempt to provide for the needs of an increased population, noxious stimuli become more frequent, and exposure to them is more probable.

If we are willing to abandon the elements of a high standard of living, population increments will be less problematical. However, I suspect that the vast majority of Americans value similar standards. Thus, we should recognize that the technology to halt population growth and to regulate human numbers is available now. If employed effectively, currently existing contraceptive methods and abortion will permit Americans to match actual with desired family size; what we lack are incentives to reduce fertility to the level needed to curtail population numbers. In the provision of those incentives the legal system can, and I believe ultimately will, play a crucial role. But the legal system is almost always a reactive institution, responding to, rather than anticipating, changed conditions. It was no accident, for example, that the Supreme Court invalidated statutes prohibiting abortion in 1973 instead of in 1953.[6] The legal system will not effectively deal with the population issue through legislation and judicial decision until the American people have adopted a new philosophy regarding the nature of the world around them and thus have come to understand the implications of population numbers.

The necessity of a new philosophy appears to be inevitable, but the change will be gradual and is likely to be forced on most individuals by circumstances rather than adopted with foresight by voluntary decision. The process is undoubtedly not unique in human history; other societies have surely found themselves compelled to change their fundamental philosophical assumptions regarding the world. However, the process of change will not be easy. Strongly held values must be shed — values that are firmly entrenched in economic and social philosophy and often in religious philosophy as well. But if we are to minimize the damage to other — and in my view, more important — values, we have no choice.

## NOTES

1. Anonymous consultant to the National Science Foundation, 1981.

2. *E.g.,* Lincoln H. Day & Alice T. Day, Too Many Americans (New York: Dell, 1964).

3. *See generally* Vaida Thompson & Mark Appelbaum, Population Policy Acceptance: Psychological Determinants 82-83 (Carolina Population Center Monograph No. 20; Chapel Hill, University of North Carolina, 1974).

4. Patrick Nolan, *Size and Administrative Intensity in Nations,* 44 American Sociological Review 110 (1979).

5. *See* James Smith & Finis Welch, *No Time to Be Young: The Economic Prospects for Large Cohorts in the United States,* 7 Population and Development Review 71 (1981); Richard Freeman, *The Effect of the Youth Population on the Wages of Young Workers,* in House Select Committee on Population, 2 Consequences of Changing U.S. Population: Baby Boom and Bust, 95th Cong.,

2d Sess. 767, 775 (1978); Peter H. Lindert, Fertility and Scarcity in America 216–59 (Princeton, N.J.: Princeton University Press, 1978); Edward Hudson & Dale Jorgenson, *Energy Prices and the U.S. Economy, 1972-1976,* 18 Natural Resources Journal 877 (1978).

6. *See generally* Helen Ebaugh & C. A. Haney, *Shifts in Abortion Attitudes: 1972-1978,* 42 Journal of Marriage & the Family 491 (1980).

# INDEX

Abortion, 151–62
  and attending physician's constitutional protections, 154–55, 156, 162
  consent of parents of minor to, 158–59
  consent of pregnant woman to, 155–56
  consent of spouse to, 156–57
  and fetus as a constitutionally protected person, 153
  freestanding clinics as providers of, 161
  frequency of, 151, 157, 158, 161
  hospital performance of, as a legal requirement, 154
  notification of, to parents of minor, 158–59
  notification of, to spouse, 157–58
  public funding of, 135–36, 159–61
Age at childbearing, 118, 121, 126–27, 129
Age structure of population, 5–6

Aliens, illegal, 173–74
Aliens, legally admitted
  access of, to private employment, 168–71
  access of, to public employment, 166–68
  access of, to public financial benefits, 171–73
Attitudes toward population growth, 3, 113
  impact of, on childbearing, 113

Capitation tax, 130, 132
Childbearing
  effect of limited space on, 43, 44
  effect of noise on, 45
Child-exclusion policies in housing, 99–106
  constitutional guarantees applicable to, 100–06
  effect of, on childbearing, 99–100
  prevalence of, 99

Childlessness, voluntary, 99–100, 129
Childrearing duties
  constitutional definition of, 67–69
  sex roles and, 64–67
Cities, problems in, as a result of population growth, 28–29
Coercion as an issue in population control, 15–16
Cohabitation, 114, 118–21
Commerce clause, 76, 133–34
Compelling interest test, 58, 61, 87, 115, 119, 135–36, 142, 143–44, 152–53, 160, 166–67, 168, 170, 171–73
Constitutional law, nature of, 7–8
Cost of children and effect on childbearing, 76, 128, 141

Direct tax, 130, 131
Due process, 41, 58, 100, 104–05, 115, 119, 131, 135, 152, 159
  test of constitutionality under. *See* Compelling interest test; Reasonable basis test

Ecology, 11
Economic problems stemming from population growth, 26–28
  employment, 26–27, 178
  taxation and government revenues, 27–28
Education
  constitutional right to, 62, 142–46
  cost of, 57, 61–64
  impact of, on attitudes toward population growth, 113
Employment of women
  and fertility, 75–76, 88–90
Environment and natural resource problems stemming from population growth, 17–25
  coastal zone and ocean resources, 22–23
  land resources, 18–20
  mineral resources and energy, 23–25, 47–48
  natural disasters and weather, 25
  water, 20–21
  wildlife protection, 21–22
Equal protection, 58, 59, 60, 62, 68, 76, 77–79, 87, 89, 102–04, 117, 142–43, 159, 166
  test of constitutionality under. *See* Compelling interest test; Reasonable basis test
Establishment clause, 62–64

Family-planning perspective, 12–13

Governmental regulation as caused by population growth, 25, 178

Health problems stemming from population growth, 30–32
  environmental insults, 31–32
  food and nutrition, 30–31
High-density housing
  effect of, on childbearing, 43, 44
  effect of, on energy consumption, 47–48
Housing problems stemming from population growth, 29

Illegitimacy, 57–61, 114, 121, 158
Immigration, 4, 6, 165–74
  constitutional authority of Congress to regulate, 165–66
Income tax as a fertility control policy, 130–31

Marriage age
  effect of, on fertility, 114, 117, 118, 121
  legal minimum for, 114–18
Motivation to curtail fertility, 7, 15–16, 55, 58

Natural increase, 4

# INDEX

Nuisance
  defined, 46
  population growth and, 47

Population perspective, 13–17
Premarital pregnancy, 114, 158

Reasonable basis test, 58, 87, 102, 103–04, 116, 135, 142–43, 144, 160, 167–68, 170–71, 172–73
Replacement level fertility, 3, 5–6
Right of family to live together, 102, 104–06
Right of privacy
  childbearing and, 41–42, 58, 59, 101–04, 106, 135, 144, 152
  effect of population growth on, 41–42
  marriage and, 115–18

Sex discrimination
  fertility and, 75–76, 88–90
  legal prohibition of, 76–79, 87
Sex relations outside marriage, 114, 118–21

State action
  requirement of, for due process, 100–01, 106
  requirement of, for equal protection, 79–87, 100–01, 106
  test for, in U.S. Court of Appeals
    First Circuit, 85–86
    Second Circuit, 79–83
    Third Circuit, 83–84
    Seventh Circuit, 84–85

Taxation
  constitutional limitations on power of, 130
  constitutional source of power of, 125–26
  fertility control policy and, 125–33
  regulation of behavior and, 133
Tenth Amendment, 146–47
Total fertility rate, 4–5, 128
Tragedy of the commons
  defined, 53–54
  private ownership and, 54–55
Tuition charges in public schools, 141–47